GUIDELINES

VOL 32 / PART 1
January–April 2016

Commissioned by **David Spriggs;** *Edited by* **Lisa Cherrett**

4–24 January
Job   *Tim Davy*

25–31 January
What makes a good city?   *Elai*

1–14 February
Ephesians: taking off and landin

15 February–6 March
Luke 1—4   *David Spriggs*   53

7–20 March
Hebrews   *Robert Mackley*   75

21–27 March
Jonah   *Bill Goodman*   90

28 March–3 April
James   *Andy Angel*   98

4–17 April
1, 2 and 3 John   *Jon Riding*   106

18–24 April
Remember me: faith and dementia   *Tricia Williams*   121

25 April–1 May
Revelation 1—3   *Ian Paul*   129

The BRF Magazine   139

Guidelines © BRF 2016

The Bible Reading Fellowship
15 The Chambers, Vineyard, Abingdon OX14 3FE
Tel: 01865 319700; Fax: 01865 319701
E-mail: enquiries@brf.org.uk; Websites: www.brf.org.uk; www.biblereadingnotes.org.uk

ISBN 978 0 85746 388 3

Distributed in Australia by Mediacom Education Inc., PO Box 610, Unley, SA 5061.
Tel: 1800 811 311; Fax: 08 8297 8719;
E-mail: admin@mediacom.org.au
Available also from all good Christian bookshops in Australia.
For individual and group subscriptions in Australia:
Mrs Rosemary Morrall, PO Box W35, Wanniassa, ACT 2903.

Distributed in New Zealand by Scripture Union Wholesale, PO Box 760, Wellington
Tel: 04 385 0421; Fax: 04 384 3990; E-mail: suwholesale@clear.net.nz

Publications distributed to more than 60 countries

Acknowledgments

The New Revised Standard Version of the Bible, Anglicised Edition, copyright © 1989, 1995 by the Division of Christian Education of the National Council of the Churches of Christ in the USA. Used by permission. All rights reserved.

The Holy Bible, New International Version (Anglicised Edition), copyright © 1979, 1984, 2011 by Biblica. Used by permission of Hodder & Stoughton Publishers, an Hachette UK company. All rights reserved. 'NIV' is a registered trademark of Biblica. UK trademark number 1448790.

The Holy Bible, English Standard Version, published by HarperCollins Publishers, © 2001 Crossway Bibles, a division of Good News Publishers. Used by permission. All rights reserved.

Extracts from *CEB* copyright © 2011 by Common English Bible.

Printed by Gutenberg Press, Tarxien, Malta.

Suggestions for using *Guidelines*

Set aside a regular time and place, if possible, when you can read and pray undisturbed. Before you begin, take time to be still and, if you find it helpful, use the BRF prayer.

In *Guidelines*, the introductory section provides context for the passages or themes to be studied, while the units of comment can be used daily, weekly, or whatever best fits your timetable. You will need a Bible (more than one if you want to compare different translations) as Bible passages are not included. At the end of each week is a 'Guidelines' section, offering further thoughts about, or practical application of what you have been studying.

Occasionally, you may read something in *Guidelines* that you find particularly challenging, even uncomfortable. This is inevitable in a series of notes which draws on a wide spectrum of contributors, and doesn't believe in ducking difficult issues. Indeed, we believe that *Guidelines* readers much prefer thought-provoking material to a bland diet that only confirms what they already think.

If you do disagree with a contributor, you may find it helpful to go through these three steps. First, think about why you feel uncomfortable. Perhaps this is an idea that is new to you, or you are not happy at the way something has been expressed. Or there may be something more substantial—you may feel that the writer is guilty of sweeping generalisation, factual error, theological or ethical misjudgment. Second, pray that God would use this disagreement to teach you more about his word and about yourself. Third, think about what you will do as a result of the disagreement. You might resolve to find out more about the issue, or write to the contributor or the editors of *Guidelines*.

To send feedback, you may email or write to BRF at the addresses shown opposite. If you would like your comment to be included on our website, please email connect@brf.org.uk. You can also Tweet to @brfonline, using the hashtag #brfconnect.

Writers in this issue

Tim Davy teaches Biblical Studies and Mission at Redcliffe College in Gloucester. His PhD was on a missional reading of Job, and he is particularly interested in the missional interpretation of the Bible.

Elaine Graham is Grosvenor Research Professor of Practical Theology at the University of Chester and Canon Theologian at Chester Cathedral. Her most recent book is *Between a Rock and a Hard Place: Public Theology in a Post-Secular Age* (SCM, 2013).

Nick Spencer is Research Director at Theos, a Christian think tank working in the area of religion, politics and society. He is the author most recently of *Atheists: The Origin of the Species* (Bloomsbury, 2014).

David Spriggs has retired from Bible Society but continues his work with them as a consultant. His main role is as a team minister at the Hinckley Baptist Church, with special responsibility to work with the leaders.

Robert Mackley read history and theology at Cambridge University before ordination. Fr Robert is currently Vicar of Little St Mary's, Cambridge. He is a published church historian and a regular columnist and reviewer for the *Church Times*.

P.W. (Bill) Goodman encourages and enables lifelong learning among fellow clergy in the Anglican Diocese of Lincoln, as Continuing Ministerial Development Officer. He has been part of ministry training courses in the UK and overseas, and currently teaches at the Lincoln School of Theology.

Andy Angel is Vice Principal of St John's College, Nottingham, and an Anglican priest. He is currently researching and writing an introduction to angels in second temple Jewish literature and early Christianity.

Jon Riding is a theologian and church musician and has been involved with Bible translation for almost 30 years as a computational linguist. He currently works with United Bible Societies, leading the Glossing Technology Project.

Tricia Williams has been writing and developing Bible resources for many years, most recently BRF's *The Gift of Years* for older people. She is the author of the 'Being with God' series (published by Scripture Union), a Bible and prayer guide designed especially for those with dementia.

Ian Paul is Associate Minister at St Nic's Nottingham, and Honorary Assistant Professor at the University of Nottingham, as well as Managing Editor at Grove Books in Cambridge. He blogs at www.Psephizo.com.

David Spriggs writes...

From Epiphany to Easter and beyond! These four months' notes cover a very eventful time in the church's year. At first glance they may not appear to offer obviously relevant material, but I invite you to look again. In addition to the obvious link with Luke 1—4 of the early days and years of Jesus' life, Luke's Gospel is focused on 'revealing' Jesus to a Gentile audience. The book of Job is also about an epiphany to a non-Israelite and its transforming impact on his life. Under the skilful guidance of Tim Davy, the missional value of this old text is laid out for us.

Before Easter, Nick Spencer explores the theologically dense text of Ephesians, which resonates with the resurrection before opening up into very challenging ethical and social topics. Robert Mackley adds colour and insight by engaging with Hebrews, which focuses so much on the priesthood of Jesus. He successfully rescues 'Melchizedek' and references to angels and tabernacle from the threat of obscurity through his perceptions and lively style.

The book of Jonah occupies us through Holy Week. This is appropriate not only because Jesus refers to Jonah as emblematic of his own death and resurrection, but because Jonah deals with the struggles involved in fulfilling God's purposes of redemption. We are grateful to Bill Goodman for elucidating this material for us. James, the brother of Jesus, was profoundly affected by the resurrection (1 Corinthians 15:7), and Andrew Angel helps us engage with his letter in the following week. Andrew shares how this material represents the teaching of Jesus in a post-resurrection context.

Jon Riding introduces us to the profound material of the Johannine epistles. Here we have an emphasis on the qualities of true belief, Christian love and intimate relationship with God through Christ.

We also have two topical sets of notes. Elaine Graham offers penetrating observations on the role of cities and the way faith in God can help to shape our lives together. Tricia Williams sensitively explores the impact of dementia, to suggest ways in which scripture can become a resource for all involved in living with this challenge.

Finally, as we approach Ascension Day, Ian Paul unpacks the insight of the glorified Christ for the seven churches of Asia Minor and for ourselves. As he says, 'The vision of Jesus is multifaceted, and different aspects of the truth about him will be relevant in different times and places.'

I pray that you will hear what the Spirit is saying to the churches, through this issue's rich offerings.

The BRF Prayer

Almighty God,
you have taught us that your word is a lamp for our
feet and a light for our path. Help us, and all who
prayerfully read your word, to deepen our
fellowship with you and with each other through your love.
And in so doing may we come to know you more fully,
love you more truly, and follow more faithfully in
the steps of your son Jesus Christ, who lives and
reigns with you and the Holy Spirit,
one God for evermore. Amen.

Job

Reading the book of Job can be a formidable experience. Although it focuses on a very specific person and situation it is in fact about everyone and for everyone. How are we supposed to live faithfully in a fallen world that is so full of fragility and brokenness? Indeed, what does faithfulness look like in the midst of pain and confusion, whether our own or that of others? As Marvin Pope puts it, the book of Job 'speaks to and for all humanity' (*Job: Introduction, Translation and Notes*, p. xxxviii).

And what does this mean for the church's participation in the mission of God? What does Job allow us, encourage us, or even require us to express as we seek to be instruments of God's good news to a world so tragically marked by sin and (often unexplained) suffering? Can wrestling with the book of Job lead the church to a more authentic, sensitive and compelling witness?

There is much that is unclear about the origins of the book. Although probably written towards or during the time of Israel's exile in Babylon, the events it describes are set in (pre-)patriarchal times and, crucially, outside of Israel. This means we won't hear much about important Israelite terms such as law, covenant, temple, exodus and so on. Thus, the author emphasises the universal relevance of his teaching and digs more deeply into the most fundamental depths of our relationship with God. These are crucial things when dealing with such a painful and universal experience as unexplained suffering.

Ultimately, the book of Job seeks to move the reader (indeed, humanity) to the realm of wisdom and an encounter with the living God. It is, therefore, a deeply practical book and one that requires our attention as individuals and as the community of God's people, seeking to bring his message of hope to the world.

Quotations are taken from the English Standard Version of the Bible, unless they are my own translation.

1 Introducing Job

Job 1:1–5

The book opens with a description of its central human character, with whom the reader will spend so much time. But what do we find out about Job and how will this prepare us for reading the rest of the book that bears his name?

First, he lived outside of Israel in the land of Uz, probably meaning he was a non-Israelite, although the events in the book appear to be set in or before the time of Abraham. Most likely, Uz refers to Edom, a brother-nation to the south-east of Israel, known for its wisdom and with multiple, albeit troubled, connections to Israel's family history (as reflected in texts such as Genesis 36 and the book of Obadiah).

Secondly, we are told his name. While we should be careful not to assume that the meaning of biblical names is always relevant, it does at least appear to be suggestive here. 'Job' could mean something along the lines of 'persecuted one' or 'where is the [divine] father?', both of which could be related to the book's themes.

Thirdly, Job's remarkable character is described. From four key attributes highlighted in verse 1, we learn that Job was a man of the utmost integrity and morality. His character was one of straightness and honourableness, marked by a true reverence for God that worked itself out in terms of his devotion to God and his dealings with people. Nobody in the Old Testament is described with the same combination of these praiseworthy terms, so Job is a very special individual indeed.

Fourthly, we read about the wholeness or *shalom* of Job's life. The numbers of children and animals seem to imply a sense of completeness (compare 1 Samuel 2:5, where the symbolic number 'seven' is used), and so the author depicts Job's life as fulfilled and thoroughly good, capped off with a reminder of his religious devotion. His was the 'good life': integrity, wealth and family *shalom*.

Some have suggested that Job's depiction is a bit too good to be true, that it is so over-the-top as to invite suspicion. This seems unnecessary to me. Here we have a description of a man (indeed, *the* man) who has everything. However, he who has everything has everything to lose.

2 Is our relationship with God a sham?

Job 1:6–12

Perhaps when you read about Job's piety and prosperity you wondered whether and how these two features of Job's life were linked. Was the good life Job enjoyed a reward for the good life he exhibited? Did these rewards provide the motivation for leading a good life in the first place?

In 1:6–12 the action shifts to heaven where God meets with members of his angelic 'government'. Included among the angelic beings is a mysterious figure called Satan, literally 'the accuser' (the Hebrew for which, *hassatan*, is a title rather than a personal name). The accuser's role, it seems, was to roam around the earth checking on the integrity of human beings.

Job becomes the subject of a discussion between God and the accuser as to whether Job worships God simply for who he is, or whether he does so for what he can get out of it. 'Of course Job serves you,' the accuser says. 'You have given him every reason to by protecting and providing for him!' (1:9–10, my paraphrase.)

The question in 1:9, 'Does Job fear God for no reason?', thus sets the direction of the entire book. Is God inherently worthy of our worship, or can he only purchase our praise by ensuring protection and prosperity? If the accuser's suspicion is correct, then the divine–human relationship would be shown to be a sham, in the order of a shallow business transaction.

And what would this mean for the mission of God? To what would God's mission be restoring humanity, if not a genuine relationship of deep trust and love? If the accuser is right, the mission of God would be pointless, leading to the most devastating version of the story of the emperor's new clothes.

Now the question has been asked, it must be answered. And the stakes could not be higher. Unwittingly, Job becomes a test case for the very integrity of the divine-human relationship. This is no longer Job's story alone; Job now represents humanity. If Job were to experience a reversal of fortunes, would he curse God to his face, or would he continue to worship? And this prompts the question we must all ask of ourselves: what would *we* do?

3 When disaster falls...

Job 1:13—2:10

To explore the integrity of human piety (or divine worthiness) the accuser is twice given permission to strike Job's *shalom*. First, in 1:13–19, Job receives overlapping reports of a series of disastrous losses of his wealth and, tragically, his children. In 2:7 we then read that the accuser attacks Job himself with painful sores all over his body. We, the readers, know these will not lead to Job's death (compare 2:6) but he does not.

There is much that could be explored in these sections but let's focus on Job's responses to these events.

To the first series of disasters, Job's response is to go into mourning but also to go into worship (1:20–21). Of the second, responding to his wife's pleading to let go and die, he asks, 'Shall we receive good from God, and shall we not receive evil/disaster?' (2:10, my paraphrase).

At first glance Job seems to meet both sets of calamity with admirable and unshakeable faith and trust. His knee-jerk response to these disasters seems to be acceptance and praise. And this is often the lesson drawn from Job for those of us who face difficulties, suffering and grief, and therefore what we think a watching world needs to see for an authentic witness

However some writers have suggested we may be able to detect hints of a movement within Job by the end of chapter 2. His second response seems less certain (it is a question rather than a statement) and less personal (he uses the generic term 'God' rather than the personal name 'Yahweh'/'the Lord'). Even the narrator adds an element of ambiguity: 'Job did not sin with his lips' (2:10) the second time. Perhaps, then, Job's initial reaction is giving way and we are beginning to witness his subtle unravelling, which becomes so evident in the following chapters.

This would certainly help to explain the change in Job's tone and temperament between the prologue and the rest of the book. I think it also opens up the possibility (indeed, necessity) of allowing for different, even contrasting, ways of responding to calamity.

4　The silence and the shouting

Job 2:11—3:26

Job is joined by three friends, Eliphaz, Bildad and Zophar. Like Job, their origins are a little ambiguous but there do seem to be at least some connections with the Genesis genealogies and Edom (see Genesis 36). Some time must have elapsed between the catastrophes and their arrival: they hear the news, travel and meet to discuss what they are to do and then make their way to Job in order to comfort him. Upon arrival they are greatly distressed with the state in which they find Job. While these friends are known best for how much they will speak later in the book, they enter Job's story in weeping and then silence for a whole week.

Meanwhile, Job has been processing and brooding over all he has experienced. As the prologue gives way to the poetic section of the book, so Job's silence gives way to anger. In his poem 'Funeral Blues', an expression of grief, W.H. Auden declares that sun, moon and stars are no longer needed; in a similar vein, Job calls for the collapse or reversal of creation ('Let there be darkness…', 3:4, my paraphrase), at least in relation to his conception and birth. Such painful self-absorption (even hubris), it seems, is the result of one's own world collapsing. How can the world carry on when we have been dealt such a devastating blow?

Job moves on to lament in verses 11–26 with a series of 'why?' questions. Why wasn't he spared his life of suffering by dying at birth? His view of Sheol (the place occupied by the dead) is rather rose-tinted, emphasising its peace relative to the sufferings of life. We also see Job shifting between himself and wider humanity as he struggles with the desirability of death over troublesome life. Job is clear: death is better than life because life is so hard.

The protective 'hedge' criticised by the accuser in 1:10 is now a cause of trouble to Job (3:23); it stops him slipping away into the release of death. As often happens to those in grief, Job's losses make him feel lost.

5 Eliphaz opens his mouth

Many have commented on how well Job's friends do initially. As we saw, they arrive and mourn and wait with Job. However in chapters 4—5 the lead comforter, Eliphaz the Temanite, decides it is time to speak. Indeed, if we discount Job's soliloquy in chapter 3, Eliphaz's speech initiates three rounds of speeches by the friends, interspersed with the words of Job as well, that stretch up to chapter 27.

In the next three studies we will dip into speeches by each of the three friends to gain a taste of themes and methods of their approaches to Job. However, in order to understand both Job and his friends, we must first understand a fundamental assumption they all make: the so-called 'retribution principle'. Put simply, this was a deeply held belief in the ancient world that a person's fortunes (health, fertility, prosperity and so on) were all directly related to their religious devotion. We have seen this idea reflected already in the suspicions of the accuser in chapter 1. If people were faithful to their god(s), they would be rewarded. Therefore, suffering was seen as the evidence of wicked or negligent behaviour.

We see this in the DNA of Eliphaz's first speech. The 'fool' (a moral category in Old Testament wisdom) gets his comeuppance (vv. 2–5) and the wicked are frustrated (vv. 12–14). Likewise, God vindicates the weak and innocent (vv. 15–16) and will restore Job's life to *shalom* if he will accept the discipline God has placed upon him (vv. 17–27).

Eliphaz is conciliatory, trying to encourage his friend, but also assuming the onus is on Job to accept his presumed punishment from God so that he may be restored.

There are elements of truth in what Eliphaz says (compare v. 17 with Proverbs 3:11–12), but he seems to be misapplying or over-applying general truths to Job's specific situation. It is as if Eliphaz's mechanical assumptions cannot accommodate challenges that reach beyond them.

In counselling Job with a neat application of the retribution principle, is Eliphaz trying to help Job or ease his own fears? This helpful idea is suggested by Carol Newsom in her commentary on Job in *The New Inter-*

preter's Bible. Comforters beware! It is a deeply troubling thing to come alongside someone on the ash-heap because it exposes in us the fear that we too could end up there. It is easier to keep asserting the status quo than consider new and troubling possibilities.

6 Bildad's turn

Job 8

Job clearly doesn't think much of Eliphaz's suggestions and declares in chapters 6–7 that his complaint is real, his friends are callous and he is without hope.

Bildad counters Job with a strong statement of the retribution principle. It simply cannot be, he says, that God would pervert justice and so, for example, Job's children must have deserved what happened to them (vv. 3–4). As for Job, on the assumption that he has sinned, if he turns to God for mercy he can be restored (vv. 5–7, 20–22).

Bildad's authority, as he perceives it, comes from tradition (vv. 8–10). This is the orthodoxy of former generations who have observed the way things work in the world and, in his view, confirm the principle of retribution. After all, who are we to question what has been passed down from generation to generation? Who is a single person to question the consensus arrived at by countless others? Is Bildad, too, fearful of challenges to the comfort of the status quo?

In verses 11–19 Bildad illustrates his point with examples of the wisdom sayings passed on by those generations. Those who dismiss God will fade like plants not properly rooted. Life is fragile and to trust in anything other than God is a precarious enterprise indeed.

Bildad concludes his first speech by assuring Job that God will lift up the righteous in the end. Although he doesn't directly accuse Job of wrongdoing there is an ambiguity in what he is saying. Unlike his children, Job still has the opportunity to put things right, and if he does he can look forward to God's blessing in the future.

One of the purposes of the book of Job was to tackle the established and incredibly harmful mechanical application of the retribution principle. It is hard to argue against tradition but what choice did Job have?

As Gerald Wilson puts it, 'The book of Job honors the quest of the one against the many. Throughout, it respects Job's struggle to know and understand, and the end of the book particularly vindicates this (42:7–9)' (*Job*, p. 77).

Guidelines

What if the accuser's question in 1:9 were asked of us? Do I worship God for who he is, or do I serve him for what I get out of it? This profound and uncomfortable question is difficult to answer. Nevertheless, the book of Job challenges us to consider the very heart of our faith as an ongoing part of our discipleship. We might also consider what this means for our Christian witness. Are we introducing people to the God who wills to be known through Jesus Christ, or do we focus on what God can do for people? They are closely linked, of course, but do we emphasise the gift or the giver?

Another aspect to reflect upon from the first week of studies is the nature of a 'faithful' response to suffering, and how we walk with others through dark times. When someone in our church community is faced with some kind of calamity, we often ask, 'How are they doing?' While the question is undoubtedly coming from a place of good concern, the book of Job challenges us to think behind and beyond the way it is phrased. Is there a 'right' answer to the question? If someone is struggling and angry, is this a worse response than if they are serenely accepting what has happened?

We have seen that Job's story seems to allow for different legitimate responses to suffering. Indeed it reflects the common experience that people's processing of pain will be complex and varied. So, do we allow room for this kind of processing in our Christian communities? If not, how can we do this practically?

Perhaps some feel that to show anger and confusion would be a 'bad witness' to those who do not share our faith. But could we say the witness of the church would be more compelling if we demonstrated that lament and complaint are part of (and not opposed to) a vibrant life of faith?

1 Zophar's perspective

Job 11

Following Bildad's first words, Job delivers an evocative speech in which he laments the hopelessness of his cause and the wretchedness of his life (look out for the subversion of Psalm 139 in Job 10, where Job seems to twist the Psalmist's awe at God's attentiveness in the womb, viewing it instead as further evidence of cruelty).

In chapter 11 the third comforter gives his opening attempt to recalibrate Job's faith along more orthodox, comfortable lines. Zophar appears less patient than his two counterparts, accusing Job of empty and foolish words (vv. 2–3). He considers Job deluded in his claims to innocence and wishes God would speak to him and disclose his wisdom (vv. 4–6), which he does in the end, although not quite in the way Zophar was anticipating. With the gloves off, the sucker punch comes in verse 6: God hasn't punished Job as much as he deserves!

In verses 7–10 Zophar illustrates the vast difference between the wisdom of God and the wisdom of humanity. In language that anticipates passages such as chapter 28 and Yahweh's speeches, Zophar declares the unsearchable extremities of God's wisdom. In his mind, Job can't possibly claim the things he does because there is too much room for saying, 'Well, I just don't know…' In fact, the book of Job as a whole seems to allow and even encourage us to hold what we know and what we don't know in tension.

God, says Zophar, will certainly not ignore sin, and he is convinced that Job is guilty. But just as Zophar seems to have given up on Job, he hands him a ray of hope. Like Eliphaz and Bildad before him, Zophar urges Job to put things right. If Job gets rid of the iniquity and injustice so evidenced by his current suffering, he will be restored and enjoy life and hope once again, in contrast with those who continue in their wickedness (vv. 13–20).

And so we see in the three comforters different aspects of the same basic position: the ordering of the cosmos revolves around God's commitment to the retribution principle; there is no room for Job's protestations of innocence: he *must* have some things in his life that have led to his suffering; Job needs to accept this teaching affirmed by the generations and turn towards God, who can restore him.

2 Voicing pain

Job 16

Imagine someone uttered the words of Job 16 in a testimony time at your church. How would you or the congregation respond?

Job's rage is in full flow and he takes out his anger on both his comforters and God. In verses 1–6 he dismisses his comforters' words as miserable platitudes. He has heard it all before and it doesn't work in his situation.

Job then turns his attention to the one whom he considers to be the true source of his pain. In causing Job's suffering, God has frustrated Job and made those around him appalled at him. Because of the belief in retribution God's treatment of Job has led to the false testimony or assumption that Job has been wicked (vv. 7–11). Job paints God as a violent and vicious adversary who tears him apart, leaving him in despair, despite his tears and prayers (vv. 12–17).

Job appeals to the earth in desperation for his cries and his case to be heard (v. 18). But who is the witness in heaven in verse 19? (See also 9:33; 19:23–27.) Traditionally, this is often read messianically, as referring to Jesus, who is described in the New Testament as having a role of advocacy in heaven (1 John 2:1). Other suggestions include God himself or Job's own cry from verse 18, which reaches heaven and testifies to Job's just cause. It is simply not at all clear what Job is referring to, so we must be careful not to load too much theological freight on to such a verse.

Returning to the situation posed at the start of today's study, it is interesting to note that by the end of the book Job is vindicated, despite the kinds of accusations he has made of God. It seems to me that, just like the psalms of lament, Job allows, enables and encourages us to voice our pain as part of the process of resolving it.

3 Where is God?

What is the church's responsibility towards the poor? I believe one of the aspects of the church's mission must be to tell the story of the poor to ourselves, to others and, crucially, to God. This is what Job is doing in chapter 24. The friends have casually reiterated their commitment to the retribution principle whereby the wicked will be punished and the poor rescued. But Job has challenged them on it. He looks around the world and sees with great distress and vexation that it doesn't seem as if God's vindicating work is actually being carried out.

Interestingly it seems only now, post-calamities, is Job able to see these vexing situations with such intensity. His pain has provided a lens through which to see the pain of others in a new and more urgent way. As Nicholas Wolterstorff put it, 'I shall look at the world through tears. Perhaps I shall see things that dry-eyed I could not see' (*Lament for a Son*, Eerdmans, 1987, p. 26).

Job 24:1–13 is utterly heart-rending and illustrates that the abuse of the poor is both an ancient and a contemporary phenomenon. The wicked exert their power by removing means of subsistence and survival by the poor (vv. 2–3). The poor are dehumanised and marginalised by being forced away from mainstream society, foraging for food like animals (vv. 4–6). They lack basic necessities for anything other than the most meagre of existences (vv. 7–8, 10). They are unable to prevent their own children being snatched away through debt (v. 9). They are exploited in order for the wealthy to gain further riches (vv. 10–11). And yet, declares Job, God seems to stand by and do nothing (vv. 1, 12).

This is not the whole story of poverty but I think it raises a crucial point. As part of his wrestling with God, Job highlights the plight of the poor. He laments the harsh ways they are treated and cries out to God for vindication of their abuse. Job's own experiences of suffering seem to have sharpened his focus as he considers the plight of others.

4 Where can wisdom be found?

It is not entirely clear whether this famous speech is Job's or someone else's, such as the author/editor of the book. The immediate context seems to imply a continuation of Job's words and there is certainly no explicit indication of a change in voice. For what it's worth, I think it is either a speech by Job or an editorial reflection of the person who put the book together. Either way, however, the topic is clearly 'wisdom' (that is, a practical understanding enabling a person to negotiate life successfully), which is addressed in three main sections.

Verses 1–11 meditate on the efforts and ingenuity of humankind in their pursuit of precious metals. These valuable commodities were known across the ancient world, including places like Egypt and the southern part of the Arabian peninsula (the probable location of Sheba and possibly also of Ophir). We have, the poem suggests, displayed mastery over creation when it comes to rooting out items of great beauty and value. No matter where they are hidden, we will find them. So surely we should be able to apply those same skills and effort to the attainment of wisdom?

Verses 12–19 declare a resounding 'No!' Although part of the DNA of creation (see, for example, Proverbs 8) wisdom and understanding/insight simply cannot be 'dug up' and traded as if they were commodities. We cannot detect wisdom on our own, and even if we could we wouldn't understand its true value, which is immeasurably greater than all the precious riches of the world. So is there any hope for those seeking wisdom?

The final section, verses 20–28, gives us hope in the form of a 'map' to wisdom. The subtle rewording of the key question in verse 20 (from 'be found' to 'come') may imply something transformative in our understanding of the nature of wisdom: 'Wisdom is no longer a commodity waiting to be found, but a dynamic, living force that comes in its own time to those who know how to receive it' (Wilson, *Job*, p. 308). It is God himself who knows the true path to wisdom and so it is in relationship with God that we too may find it (v. 28).

This is the compelling message of biblical wisdom for the people of God, and also for the world.

5 A lament for the past

Job 29

Following his reflection on the nature of wisdom in chapter 28, Job begins a final and lengthy speech in which he recalls the past (ch. 29), dwells on the present (ch. 30), and attempts to move ahead into the future (ch. 31). The three main comforters have had their say and Job now sums up his defence.

Job laments his lost life of *shalom* in which he experienced the pleasure and blessing of God, seen not least in his family wholeness (vv. 2–6, 18–20). He had incomparable social standing and influence in the community, inspiring awe even among princes and nobles (vv. 7–11, 21–25).

As is often the case in Hebraic writing, the focus of the passage is in the middle section, in this case verses 12–17. Here Job explains the reasons why he was so esteemed: he had a firm grasp of, indeed he embodied, the core values of righteousness and justice. As such, this passage is in part a lament and in part a defence of his integrity.

Job did not exploit his influence and power but lived out the values of righteousness and justice that are intrinsic to who God is and what he wants for his people and his world (see Genesis 18:17–19; Deuteronomy 10:12–22, which are two examples of God's commitment to justice and righteousness being reflected upon in the context of shaping his people). He acted on behalf of the vulnerable and needy, addressing their cries for help, giving them justice and hope. He matched their loss by protecting, providing and vindicating. He even sought out justice for those outside his sphere of direct responsibility and took action against those exploiting the poor.

Job did not merely carry out acts of righteousness and justice; he lived them. He embodied them so that he could say, in verse 14, 'I put on righteousness and it clothed itself with me; my justice was like a robe and a turban' (my translation). It seems to me this is a high point in Old Testament ethics. Here we have the portrait of an ideally ethical person who lives and breathes God's righteousness and justice—some might say, incarnates it. As such Job's defence asks profound questions about the way that we, the church, live out God's rule in our lives and communities.

6 Pointed pain

Job 30

From the past to the present; from riches and respect to rags and ridicule. Despite his life of integrity, Job's social standing has reversed. No longer causing the awe and silence of princes and nobles, Job is now the butt of jokes by ruffians and reprobates (vv. 1–15). It is not just in our own day that someone could go from adulation one minute to mockery the next. To use a contemporary idiom, Job's fall from adulation has gone viral.

Verses 16–23 provide vivid insight into Job's state of mind in relation to Yahweh. He places the cause of his deep distress and physical agony with God. Like C.S. Lewis who, in the midst of grief, found 'A door slammed in your face, and a sound of bolting and double bolting on the inside. After that, silence' (C.S. Lewis, *A Grief Observed*, p. ??), Job cries out into the air, 'Where are you?!'

Whereas the attentive presence of God is usually a sign of hope, for Job at this point it is ironic and cruel. God seems to look on impassively as Job suffers. Actually, no, says Job: God is active—active against him, persecuting him, tossing him around in a storm, ready to bring him down to death.

In the final section of the passage (vv. 24–31) Job attempts to shame God into compassionate action, but, in doing so, exposes his sense of hubris as well. In verse 25 Job points out that he himself knows what compassion looks like, having wept with the troubled in his former life of *shalom*. Job's point seems to be that he knows the right response to a person's suffering and, crucially, God seems to be ignorant or negligent in this regard. The implication here is that Job knows better than God. In claiming such, has he moved from complaint to arrogance? Does he really know better than God how affairs of the universe should be conducted? Is Job right here and in chapter 24 to claim that God is neglecting his responsibilities of governance of the universe? We will return to this theme when we reach the speeches of Yahweh.

Guidelines

As we have seen, the book of Job has much to say about how we process our pain and the pain of others. One outcome of Job's suffering is that his capacity to walk in solidarity with the poor seems to have grown. While he advocated for the weak and vulnerable in his former days, he now sees their plight from a new perspective.

The book is also profoundly challenging concerning the church's engagement with issues of poverty and justice in the contemporary world. We are called to speak on behalf of the poor, telling their stories and challenging those who exploit them. We are called to confront unhelpful ideas or downright false theologies that perpetuate the plight of the poor. In our own day, it could be argued that the 'prosperity gospel', where obedience and faith are necessarily rewarded with health and wealth, is just an extension of the retribution principle the book of Job argues so vehemently against.

We might also consider our attitudes when engaging with issues of poverty and justice. Is this arm's-length benevolence, or solidarity with God's very heart? In our communities, could we claim, like Job, to embody God's commitment to righteousness and justice?

Could we also say that the book of Job not only legitimises lament before God on behalf of the poor and the suffering, but actually requires it of God's people? Is this part of the church's priestly role before God and in the world?

A final reflection on wisdom, which will become a more dominant theme in our final week of studies. Just as the people of the ancient world were skilful and determined to dig up great treasures from the earth, so we in the contemporary world expend great ingenuity and effort to pursue wealth and other kinds of substance. How much do we yearn and search for God's wisdom?

1 Job's oaths of innocence

Job 31

Apart from his two brief responses to the divine speeches in 40:4–5 and 42:2–6, chapter 31 represents Job's final words in the book. They are the final throw of the dice for a man who is desperate for vindication, and yearning for (yet fearful of) an encounter with Yahweh (for this mixture of emotions see, for example, 9:14–20, 32–35; 23:2–17; see also Newsom, 'The book of Job', p. 595).

Job is trying to force God's hand by uttering a series of curses along the lines of 'If I have done A, then let B happen to me.' If, as a result of the curses, Job receives these punishments then it is clear that he has indeed committed the crimes assumed by the friends. If, however, nothing happens, then this proves Job's innocence. Either way, Job is hoping to bring God out of hiding.

However, chapter 31 also gives us a window into Job's ethical world and, I think, contributes to the shaping of a vision of society that is characterised by justice and righteousness. Sexual fidelity (vv. 1, 9–12), commitment to truth (vv. 5–6), rejection of the love of money or other gods (vv. 24–28) and right use of land and its workers (vv. 38–40) are a few examples, but perhaps most striking is the concentration on Job's dealings with the vulnerable in verses 13–23. Job claims that when he was a man of great wealth and power, he always treated those under his influence with integrity, whether servants in his household or the poor more generally. He held to a belief in some kind of equality between people, regardless of their social or economic position. He provided the poor with food, clothing and justice. Moreover, he joined them in hospitality and fellowship, meeting the needs of the most vulnerable in society.

As we have seen, Job is totally convinced of his integrity and, therefore, the utter inappropriateness of his sufferings. He cries out for vindication, confident that a divine testimony concerning his life would exonerate him of all charges (vv. 35–37). It is upon this hope that he rests his defence: 'The words of Job are ended' (v. 40).

Job is still clinging to the retribution principle in the way he shapes his arguments. It will take divine intervention to move the debate into the arena of wisdom where the mechanics of retribution no longer apply in the same way. But before the word from Yahweh, we must hear one more human perspective.

2 Elihu interrupts

Job 36

The cycle of speeches between Job and his friends in chapters 3—31 has concluded, some would say, rather messily. Bildad's third speech seems to have been cut short (25:1–6) and Zophar doesn't get a third speech at all. While many scholars have attempted to rearrange the material in the third cycle (chs 22—27) I prefer the view that the untidy ending is an indication of the breakdown in the debate. Seeing that they have not convinced Job, the friends have run out of ideas and run out of steam.

We then hear Job's final defence and would now expect to hear God's definitive word. But instead a new character enters the fray. Elihu is a younger man who is frustrated with the failure of the friends to change Job's perspective. His section (a full six chapters) has the effect of delaying God's speeches, thus building the tension and perhaps preventing it looking as if God is responding too quickly to Job's demands in chapter 31. Elihu also uses creation language that anticipates God's speeches, which builds a nice bridge to that conclusive section of the book (see especially ch. 37). We will take chapter 36 as a sample of Elihu's approach.

Rather arrogantly, Elihu claims to have definitive and perfect knowledge that sets him over and against Job, whom he sees as in the wrong (vv. 1–4). He reaffirms a form of the retribution principle whereby God punishes the wicked and vindicates the righteous, which, he suggests, illustrates the might and wisdom of God (vv. 5–15). Crucially, Elihu sees a redemptive opportunity in suffering in that God speaks to the afflicted through their affliction (v. 15). Therefore, Job should be careful not to let his affliction distract him from the proper course of action—that is, repentance (vv. 16–21).

Elihu then rounds off the chapter with a meditation on the great-ness and creativity of God. He is the ultimate power and teacher in the universe and cannot be contradicted (a dig at Job, perhaps, but also an ironic statement coming from his own confident representation of God's views). There is a chasm between our understanding and God's. And, as the final verses demonstrate through the imagery of storms and lightning (common imagery for divine beings in the ancient world), God is ultimately 'other'.

3 Yahweh's first speech

Job 38—39

At last, Job receives what he has asked for, yet feared as well: an encoun-ter with Yawheh. God's two speeches are critical for our understanding of the book as a whole and lead to its ultimate resolution. Scholars have detected different tones to the speeches (are they harsh and sarcastic or playful?), but David Clines warns us wisely that tone is often very cultur-ally specific and, for modern readers, there is no way of being certain.

Job stands before God in his own suffering but, as we have seen, also occupies an 'everyman' role, representing the whole of humanity in our confusion and pain. The response God gives to Job, then, is not just for Job but for us all. Yet in his speeches Yahweh both answers and doesn't answer Job.

Job does not find out why his suffering happened. He is not (yet) assured that he will be vindicated and restored. Indeed, the speeches are not about Job at all.

Crucially, Yahweh moves the debate away from the tightly defined arena of retribution in which the friends and Job have been operating and where a mechanical rule of cause and consequence reigns supreme. Instead, Yahweh moves the debate into the arena of creation and wis-dom (as has been hinted at in earlier sections such as chapter 28 and Elihu's speeches), an arena in which only he is qualified to operate.

All the human characters in the book have spoken presumptuously in one way or another, but the focus here is on Job speaking about things he understands inadequately. Through a seemingly relentless series of questions, Yahweh asks Job if he really thinks he is qualified to understand how the universe works and, therefore, how it should be governed. The questions range around the creation, with little reference to humanity, taking in, among other things, the stars, various forms of water and a host of different animals.

What ties these vastly different elements together is God's wisdom in creating them and knowing their intimate details. Perhaps we can also detect God's sheer delight in creation and its wildness. God understands the workings of those aspects of creation that are beyond human fathoming.

4 Yahweh continues...

Job 40—41

Following Job's brief and rather non-committal response to the first speech in 40:4–5, Yahweh challenges his presumptuousness again (40:8) and focuses his attention on two particularly fearsome and wild creatures: Behemoth and Leviathan. These have been identified both as normal animals (usually the hippopotamus and crocodile, respectively) and as mythical creatures of chaos, especially with reference to other ancient Near Eastern ideas. Perhaps there is room for both identities. In any case, what is most instructive is to see which attributes of these beasts are picked up on by God, and how these underline his point in relation to the themes of Job. This might help us to answer George Bernard Shaw, who claimed, 'If I complain that I am suffering unjustly, it is no answer to say, "Can you make a hippopotamus?"'

Behemoth (40:15–24) is characterised by frightening strength and power. He is preeminent among the animals listed so far in the speeches. In 40:24 Yahweh asks Job whether anyone could tame Behemoth. No: he is too strong, too powerful, too wild. He is untameable, reflecting those elements in creation that are beyond human control.

Leviathan enjoys an extensive meditation. Again, the question is asked, 'Job, can you tame this beast?' (41:1–10). Of course not: Leviathan is beyond human control, strong, fearsome, wild and dangerous. God is making the point that there are plenty of aspects to creation beyond our horizons. There is much more to it than a human-centred view. Secondly, in the helpful words of Gerald Wilson, 'it is as impossible for humans to bind "leviathan" to fulfil human will as it is to capture and control God himself. Ultimately, "leviathan" is a powerful symbol to Job (and the reader) of a world (and a God!) outside human control' (*Job*, p. 460).

We might also pause to consider the way these verses inform the creation-care issue, which is such an important topic for the church to engage with. As Richard Bauckham observes in his excellent book *Bible and Ecology*, the Yahweh speeches put humanity in our place. Also, how would our approach to environmental care be improved if we were soaked in God's sheer delight for his creation?

5 Job reconsiders

Job 42:1–6

Job thought he understood how the universe was governed, or should be governed. He concluded, via the retribution principle, that Yahweh was not keeping up his end of the bargain forged between God and humanity. Yet now he has been blasted by the overwhelming wisdom and power of God, who delights in his creation with all of its untamed elements and extremities, much of which goes on quite apart from human beings.

The meaning of the words in Job's 'confession' in 42:2–6 are notoriously difficult to pin down, the climax of which (v. 6) may be rendered along the lines of 'Therefore I submit and recant concerning dust and ashes.' What does seem clear is that Job accepts the wisdom of God and his freedom to act how he wishes. As if in a court of law, Job withdraws his own complaints on the grounds of what he now recognises as his insufficient capacity to know what is going on.

Job's encounter with Yahweh has been transformative. He has been put in his place and, therefore, so has humanity. But this meeting has been one not simply of rebuke, but of a deepening relationship.

It is also worth considering that, unlike those familiar with his book, Job does not know the end of his story. He withdraws his accusations and accepts the freedom and wisdom of God, not knowing whether or how this will affect his life. For all he knows, his life will continue on the ash heap.

And that is the point. In being confronted with the scale and complexity of creation, and the enormity of God's wisdom, Job recalibrates his view of himself (and of humanity) and accepts that, ultimately, we cannot know how the universe works, let alone dictate to God how it should be governed. Equally, we will only find a way along the path through pain by entrusting ourselves to Yahweh, regardless of what may lie ahead. This, it seems, is one way to answer George Bernard Shaw's objection to the speeches, and shows the heart of the 'true' answer to our questions.

6 Back to normality?

Job 42:7–17

Is the conclusion to Job's story a rather anticlimactic way to end such a profound and probing exploration? Following Job's retraction in 42:2–6, the book's epilogue returns to a prose style and recounts Job's restoration to prosperity and *shalom*. Indeed, his wealth ends up being double what it had been!

So is this a reward for Job's righteousness and for proving the accuser wrong? If so, doesn't this undermine the whole premise of the book? Isn't it a return to the retribution principle that good behaviour is rewarded, and vice versa?

As we have seen, Job did not know he would be rewarded at all, let alone to the staggering extent set out in the epilogue, so this couldn't have been a motivation. Perhaps more important is that Job's restoration and blessing illustrates the freedom of God to act however he desires. The blessing of Job here is not the fulfilment of an obligation on God's part but an act of sovereignty and love. He blesses because he desires to bless.

In verses 7–9 God deals with the three main comforters, vindicating Job in their sight. Job has spoken what is right and they have not. Although Job was operating with false assumptions throughout the book, and speaking out of ignorance, there was still something 'right' about him. Perhaps God is declaring that Job's honest struggling was a truer response than glib and partial answers. In any case, the tables are turned and it is now Job who must help the comforters, praying on their behalf.

The final few verses of the book portray the restoration of Job in all aspects of life: wealth, community, family and health. But a crucial difference is that he is now aware it could all be lost again. In a very real sense, as observed by William Brown in his article 'Introducing Job: A journey of transformation', Job now needs to learn how to enjoy *shalom*, knowing it isn't guaranteed. Those of us who have mourned need to learn to laugh again.

And so Job has returned to *shalom*. He is more aware of the untamed nature of living in the world, but also of the wisdom of Yahweh and his freedom to act how he wishes. Ultimately, the book of Job encourages the church in its mission to a broken world, where the only true 'answer' is an encounter with Yahweh.

Guidelines

The driving question of the book of Job was uttered by the accuser in 1:9: 'Does Job fear God for no reason?' The reader now knows that Job has been vindicated. Yes, it is possible for the divine–human relationship to be one of deep love and trust that goes beyond what we can get out of it. And so the mission of God, which has also been thrown into question, is also vindicated.

How are we to live in the light of all that has been presented in Job? Perhaps we will each have a different response to this question as we each bring different experiences of pain and confusion to our reading of the text. Although we would like the book of Job to provide neat answers to our painful questions, this would undermine the reality of our pain and that of others. There simply are no easy answers. What the book does, however, is present us with a vision of a God in whom we can encounter truth and wisdom and, in some way, be transformed. We do not have the capacity to understand how the universe works but God does.

The book prizes honesty and struggling with God in the context of a relationship with him. As in the Psalms, wrestling with God is seen as a sign of a vital faith rather than a brittle one. Faith in God therefore allows (requires!) room for honest enquiry and questioning alongside a commitment to engage with and trust God. As church we are uniquely positioned to carry out this calling before God and before the world.

FURTHER READING

William Brown, 'Introducing Job: A journey of transformation', *Interpretation*, 53.3 (1999), pp. 228–38.

David Clines, *Job*, three volumes (Thomas Nelson, 1989, 2006, 2011).

John Goldingay, *Job for Everyone* (SPCK, 2013).

Gustavo Gutiérrez, *On Job* (Orbis Books, 1987).

Tremper Longman III, *Job* (Baker Academic, 2012).

Carol Newsom, 'The book of Job', in *The New Interpreter's Bible*, Vol. 4, edited by L.E. Keck (Abingdon Press, 1996), pp. 317–637.

Marvin Pope, *Job: Introduction, Translation and Notes* (Garden City, 1965).

John Walton, *Job* (Zondervan, 2012).

Gerald Wilson, *Job* (Paternoster, 2007).

What makes a good city?

Cities have been microcosms of human life and engines of civilisation for over 6000 years. This is clearly reflected in biblical literature, which tells of humanity's gradual gravitation towards the urban from the rural, a trend that continues to the present day. While the Bible may portray the city as a place of exile, enslavement and destruction, as in Babylon, often serving as the manifestation of human voraciousness and pride, the future—as manifested in the reparative acts of God—is nevertheless still to be found in the city. Despite the countryside's attractions, humanity is asked to divest itself of rural nostalgia and embrace the city, albeit one whose proportions will far exceed urban culture's often petty and self-serving ambitions, pointing rather towards a flourishing community transformed into a place of creativity and justice.

Perhaps because of their population density and the pace of change, cities are places of extremes: despair and degradation, fear and hope, wealth and poverty, cruelty and charity. The corporate symbolism of space and place, the hubristic statements of status and power reflected in the iconic monuments of the urban skyline, the unseen flows and exchanges of wealth and human traffic are all signs of the values that underpin city living: ancient and modern, biblical and contemporary. Yet because humans live there, biblical literature has also characterised the city as a place of blessing and human endeavour, a divine dwelling-place, and a place of faithful and resilient incarnational witness. These Bible studies explore the tension between the rural and the urban, and between the city as a place of darkness and banishment and the city as a place of hope and reconciliation.

Quotations are taken from the New Revised Standard Version of the Bible.

1 Build wisely

Genesis 11:1–9

The 21st century will be an urban epoch. The United Nations has estimated that by 2020, 80 per cent of the world's population in Europe, the Americas and West Asia will live in cities; even in Africa, East Asia and Oceania, where the migration process to cities started later, the concentration will approach 50 per cent. Urban centres have always been magnets for those drawn to a better life and an escape from mere subsistence—and yet the perils of desperate poverty, social dislocation, violence and disease are also ever-present.

The future of the 21st-century city may be seen in places such as Qatar, which has (controversially) been selected to host the 2022 FIFA World Cup. The ultra-modern hotels, shopping malls and artificial beaches glisten like jewels in the desert, and flaunt the promise of an idyllic consumerist paradise. But this superficial luxury is bought at the expense of the estimated 1.4 million migrant workers who endure some of the worst conditions in the world, with low wages and widespread fatalities. The lucrative economic gains are allowed to eclipse other considerations, such as the human cost, the rumours of corruption and the questionable sporting benefits of staging a world-class competitive tournament in temperatures exceeding 40°C.

The story of the tower of Babel may be read against such snapshots of contemporary cities. It is a satire on the pretensions of monumental buildings and cosmopolitan elites. The origins of Babel reflect the transition of civilisations from nomadic or dispersed peoples to populations in permanent dwelling-places. Such great settlements are testaments to human ingenuity, but if the ambition to build exceeds human utility or sustainability, and strays into vanity projects or accumulation of wealth, status and power for their own sake, idolatry creeps in as the city itself becomes a fetish, an object of worship. The drive to build the world's tallest building or 'make a name for ourselves' (v. 4) verges on hubris. Pride in such achievement blinkers humanity to the true conditions of our creaturely existence and leads us to believe we are capable of playing God. Cities built on the logic of grand designs and technical-rational planning, underpinned by selective immigration, with people cloistered in gated communities, are symptoms of an attempt to impose a false and sterile will to power on the risk, diversity and flux of life.

2 Seek the welfare of the city

Jeremiah 29:4–14

Uprooted from the holy city of Jerusalem and exposed to the profanities of the alien nation state of Babylon, the people of Israel are instructed to build, settle, marry and work for the sake of their place of exile. Surely this represents a form of collusion—capitulation to the powers that be and resignation to the inevitability of captivity and the heresy of 'going native'. Anyone who has been forced to leave their original home for economic, political or other reasons, or who feels their own neighbourhood has taken a turn for the worse, may experience a similar sense of exile and be tempted to resist or retreat into an enclave of ex-pats or NIMBYs. The 'prophets and diviners' among the Jews in Babylon (v. 8) were perhaps those who preached resistance to assimilation and encouraged the people to seek solace in their dreams of return and restoration. What's so wrong with that? Surely this is the way a faithful people can maintain their authentic identity under threat. Surely this is the way to keep the flame of desire for liberation alive, and the passion to dwell once more in a place where true faith and old ways will be upheld without compromise. What stake can the righteous sojourner possibly have in the customs and institutions of the heathens?

Yet the counsel of Jeremiah is to cultivate faithfulness in exile, and to trust in the purposes of the Lord, whose plans for the community will be fulfilled in his own good time. Jeremiah's advice is to cultivate habits of resilience, find the virtues of the alien city within the rhythms of its own daily life, and above all not to disdain the opportunities of the present for the sake of some (imagined) greener pastures. Are the daily tasks of dwelling, planting and sowing, raising families and making a living not the same the world over? Do we not all have a stake in building, increasing and flourishing—goals that are more easily achieved and sustained when they are shared in the name of our common humanity?

When the time comes to rebuild the homeland, it is just possible that the experiences of captivity and exile will have generated a deeper wisdom—including, possibly, greater compassion towards the sojourners in their own midst and a more judicious understanding of the common good—than would have ensued if the years of banishment and dispossession had not intervened.

3 Weep for the city

Jeremiah 22:1–5, 8–17; Matthew 11:20–25

As well as calling for personal repentance, the Bible anticipates the transformation of structural, collective institutions. While it would be reductionist to ascribe a fixed personality to a place, cities are more than collections of individuals or inanimate networks of streets and buildings. They have corporate identities and play formative roles in shaping our societies, materially, spiritually and ideologically. It follows that Christian engagement with the city must involve mission and ministry that are public and institutional as well as personal and spiritual.

In the face of the city's many iniquities, it is notable that Jesus' contemplation of Chorazin, Bethsaida and Capernaum (Matthew 11:21, 23) and, later, Jerusalem (Luke 19:41–44) is less denunciation and outrage and more a spirituality of lament. The evangelist here places Jesus in the prophetic tradition, as one who contemplates the prospect of the cities as much in sorrow as in anger, and views the quality of urban life according to a God who hears the cry of the poor and marginalised. The fate of widows, orphans, sojourners and poor people at the hands of the ruling classes calls into question the integrity of any grand design. As Jeremiah observes in his denunciation of the rulers of Judah, a city built on foundations of injustice is neither secure nor sustainable (Jeremiah 22:3–5). History will bear witness to this.

This is a prophetic tradition which, in its critique of monarchical ideology, sees that ideology tangibly embodied in the urban environment. In our day, such social and economic divisions may be played out in the form of gated communities, surveillance technology, zero-hour contracts, cutbacks in public services and a lack of sustainable infrastructure. The cries of the poor and the land laid waste—whether in adulterated nature or the compromised ecology of the modern city—speak of a lack of faith with the divine covenant of justice and compassion. It is the task of the prophet to bring to speech these muted and repressed sounds of suffering, and, in speaking truth to power, to make sure these cries are heard in the public domain.

4 Keep faith with the city

Acts 1:3–8

While Christianity has its origins in the provinces of Galilee, it is in the city of Jerusalem—the centre of religious and imperial power in that region—that the decisive drama of Jesus' death and resurrection is played out. The earthly ministry of Jesus was conditioned by rural and small-town life, and those who return home after his death record encounters with the risen Christ amid the villages and fishing-boats of Galilee. Yet the disciples who remain in Jerusalem do so intentionally, and against the grain of any tendency to return to where they came from. Is the centre of gravity of the new community to be rural or urban?

Contemporary Christians are used to seeing the New Testament texts as riven with debates about the early church being predominantly Jewish or Gentile, and about the choice between wealth and poverty, or between hierarchy and equality in matters of class, status and gender. However it is possible the urban/rural divide also preoccupied the earliest generations of disciples. It would appear that, despite the jeopardy, the economic and political insecurities, the complexities of managing cultural and religious pluralism, the vocation—and eventually the eschatological imagination—of the church gradually becomes decidedly urban.

At the start of Acts, we see the disciples' growing realisation that obedience to the risen Lord impels them to remain in Jerusalem in spite of all the risks. The risen Jesus orders them to stay there to await further visitations (v. 4); and it is there, on the day of Pentecost, that the power to be witnesses will be given, through the Holy Spirit, as Jesus promises in verse 8. This gift transcends the teachings of the earthly Jesus and becomes 'good news' for a global, undivided human community.

From then on, as it disseminates throughout the Middle East, Christianity is quintessentially an urban and cosmopolitan phenomenon, conditioned by cultural diversity and geographical mobility. The vision of the heavenly city comes profoundly to shape the missionary imperative of the gospel, a vision believed to be taking shape in the corporate life of the worshipping communities who proclaim the lordship of Jesus.

5 Glimpsing the gospel

Acts 17:16–34

The book of Acts is a series of urban incidents, as Paul, Peter and others travel the Mediterranean region preaching the gospel. Here, Paul's journeys have taken him to another major centre, Athens, one that symbolises cultural and intellectual diversity.

Paul debates with pagan philosophers at the Areopagus, where he proclaims a God who is beyond human comprehension and yet prefigured in many creeds and philosophies. This is an important moment in Christian apologetics, Paul consciously adopting pagan terminology in order to communicate the groundwork of the gospel. It is helpful to remember that from its earliest missionary origins Christianity was engaging with diverse cultures and its messengers were engaging with and needing to convince pagans, Jews, Gentiles and imperial powers. This was in part a result of the extent of the Roman empire, but also a product of the urban nature of the Mediterranean region of Paul's day. The empire provided him, in particular, with easy transport links and some degree of civil protection. However it was clear that since cities were also hubs of cultural cross-fertilisation, then the gospel had to be mediated accordingly.

While contemporary apologetics is often reduced to proof-texts and logical arguments, at root it involves a step into the world view of others. Amid the pluralism and cosmopolitanism of the city, culture, philosophy and the arts give shape to our human creativity but also contain the seeds of the gospel, even though such glimpses may await their final consummation in the revelation of Christ.

Contemporary urban life presents us with a wealth of human cultural expression. Proximity of space and place offers rich opportunities to speak across the divide, if we listen carefully to the shared concerns that preoccupy public discourse. This is all about actively seeking conversation partners. Many urban churches and cathedrals have developed a ministry that consciously makes space for occasions of cultural, religious and intellectual exchange, either by offering hospitality in city-centre buildings or venturing into the marketplace of ideas. Yet if we think our generation is unique in having to address a post-Christian context of radical pluralism, or if we mourn the passing of an era in which everyone knew the basics of Bible stories, the Lord's prayer and Christian doctrine, then Acts 17 is a reminder that the gospel has always had to speak into a crowded and noisy marketplace containing many gods.

6 The new Jerusalem

Revelation 21:9—22:5

Eventually, from Jerusalem, Christianity finds its way to another imperial, economic and religious powerhouse: Rome. This casts a shadow over the apocalyptic visions of the writer of Revelation, in which the urban imagination of the early church reaches its apotheosis. So one of the gifts of the book of Revelation to the church is the vision of the redeemed creation at the end of days, as characterised by the 'holy city' (21:10), a huge megalopolis that covers the entire inhabited world.

As with much utopian or futuristic literature, might we read Revelation as both an eschatological vision and a sideways commentary on its own day? The vision of the writer of Revelation constructs an alternative, imaginary world, designed to enable readers to think the unthinkable and picture a place where there is no more hunger, want or sorrow. Its refraction of the familiar into the fantastic offers the chance to construct a prophetic yet profoundly contextualised vision of how the people of God might begin to anticipate the shape of the world to come, in and through their everyday practices of holiness, vigilance and service.

Yet the utopia is not to be realised in a flight from the urban. This future world has no outside, no rural idyll or sanctuary to which these urban Christians could retreat. The life of the world to come, and the sensibilities of those who inhabit the new creation, will be something like those of Babylon, Jerusalem and Rome all rolled into one, emerging out of their chaos, exploitation and hubris, while retaining their essential marks of pluralism, abundance and cultural exchange. The calling of the people of God is to declare and embody an alternative reality in anticipation of the world to come, the true reign of God.

Guidelines

These readings reflect a divine calling to love the city and seek its redemption, in the expectation that one day the fallen Jerusalem will be restored and transformed by God into the heavenly city. But this entails a true solidarity, a form of realism, which seeks not to escape from the compromises of the city but to engage with it in all its complexity and ambivalence. We might start by praying:

- For those in government, public policy and transport services who are responsible for managing our cities.
- For all those in our cities who are homeless, or in inadequate housing, or who struggle to survive on low incomes.
- For the cultural and artistic life of our cities: that it may nurture honesty, a sense of beauty and the celebration of common purpose.
- For all those involved in maintaining ministries of hope, justice and reconciliation in urban communities, and those exploring whether they are being called to work in urban ministry.

FURTHER READING

Dieter Georgi, *The City in the Valley: Biblical interpretation and urban theology* (Society of Biblical Literature, 2005).

Elaine Graham and Stephen Lowe, *What Makes a Good City? Public theology and the urban church* (Darton, Longman and Todd, 2009).

David Smith, *Seeking a City with Foundations: Theology for an urban world* (IVP, 2011).

Philip Sheldrake, *The Spiritual City: Theology, spirituality, and the urban* (Wiley-Blackwell, 2014).

Ephesians: taking off and landing

Over the next two weeks we will be looking at Paul's letter to the Ephesians (or most of it—we've had to omit chapter 3, which is a typical Pauline handbrake turn, for reasons of space). It's a rich, dense, sometimes difficult, often inspiring letter, probably written towards the end of Paul's life, when he was in prison in Rome. Like many of Paul's letters, it manages to achieve both a bird's eye view of God's plans for creation and humanity, and a thoroughly grounded, grass-roots, practical response for what that means—which explains the title for our fortnight's theme.

The overall theme of the letter is unity—oneness in love—and that will be a recurring idea in this study. Also the idea of taking off and coming in to land links our two weeks together—that is, how what we believe (week 1) is not incidental to how we live (week 2) but in fact very closely connected to it. Not only should our Christian trust in what God has done through Christ provide the foundations for what we do in our daily lives, but it should also (to pile up metaphors in good Pauline fashion!) be a compass, map and guide, showing us where we are going and how we should get there, and calling us back when we go wandering off on ways that seem easier and more pleasant than Christ's path.

Quotations are taken from the New International Version of the Bible.

1 Vertical take-off

Ephesians 1:1–10

No matter how often I fly, I never get tired of take-off. It's not so much the drama of acceleration and the sheer miracle of sensing 50 tonnes of metal defy gravity as those few minutes when the familiar landscape of airport, suburbs and fields tilts and reforms, then fits together. From two, then five, then 10,000 feet the world looks different. You get distance, perspective—a sense of knowing something that you didn't know on the ground.

The opening to Ephesians is a bit like that, only Paul's take-off is less of a growl down two miles of runway than it is a vertical blast-off. Having introduced himself in his customary manner, he forgoes the lengthy pleasantries of, say, his letters to the Philippians and the Colossians, and goes straight into an extraordinary—and extraordinarily dense—prayer of praise.

We are given vast perspectives—not so much from 10,000 feet as from the edge of space, and time. Straight away we are there with God 'in the heavenly realms' (v. 3), and 'before the creation of the world' (v. 4), and 'when the times reach their fulfilment' (v. 10). We are shown the towering features of the landscape—grace, predestination, forgiveness, redemption (vv. 5–7)—as the Pauline aircraft banks and, barely giving us a chance to take in what is below us, heads on.

It can be a bit confusing and even disconcerting. The point, however, is not to get unduly concerned in probing the details at this stage, but rather to note how they fit together—to notice how the full landscape of the Christian story appears from on high—and then to move on, for the time being, as Paul does. We have God's plans before the creation of the world, his action in Christ 'when the times reach their fulfilment', the resulting cosmic unity 'to all things in heaven and on earth under Christ' (v. 10), and through the whole story the love and grace and pleasure and will of God.

No matter how vast and varied the landscape looks, there is a single feature, a characteristic if you like, that is identifiable throughout, namely God's unconquerable love. Hence this theological panorama is, in typical Pauline style, a prayer—indeed an outburst—of praise. Perhaps it is the kind of feeling you get when you see the features of a landscape you love come together from 10,000 feet.

2 Predestined to be predestined?

Ephesians 1:11–14

Predestination is an idea about which much ink (and not a little blood) has been spilt. It's an idea that nags away at us, whether we are doing theology or not. Are we truly free? How much of our life, our thoughts, our future is determined by our parents? Our upbringing? Our genes? Our culture?

Nobody likes to think the answer is everything. Indeed, as people rapidly realise, it can't be everything because complete determinism saws through the branch on which it sits. If everything about me is determined, then that includes my belief in determinism, which becomes meaningless. Somehow, some way, I must be free.

At first glance, Paul, in this passage, appears to tug us away from a belief in freedom. We have been 'chosen' and 'predestined' by one who 'works out everything in conformity with the purpose of his will' (v. 11). Christians have struggled with these verses for centuries, never (to my mind, at least) reaching a completely satisfactory conclusion.

But perhaps we can edge towards an answer by returning to the metaphor of yesterday—the aeroplane's view of the big picture—and realising that Paul is still doing the big picture here. It would be a mistake to unpack a minutely detailed theology of predestination from Paul's words in this passage. Rather, we might just note their main point—that God is before, now and after, and that despite the freedom we have to make our own choices (including bad ones), God remains sovereign.

Sometimes, though (perhaps even most of the time), it can feel as if the very opposite is true: our freedom is limitless, there is no script to life at all, and we are simply left to improvise in a universe that couldn't possibly care less for us. That is not the Christian story, however. Ultimately, there is a point, there is a purpose.

Perhaps a better analogy would be that we are given not a script but an overall plot. We are chosen to be on stage and predestined to play certain roles by him who knows how the play will end. We are, if you like, determined into those roles—we cannot be anyone else. Moreover, we are shown how we should play those roles—through our conscience, through God's law, through God's personal intervention in Christ.

None of that, however, stops us from being ourselves, from being Bill or Trevor or Jane. What it does show us is what kind of self, what kind of Bill/Trevor/Jane we should be. God ultimately remains in charge of the play and of the plot: our freedom and our responsibility is to be the characters he has commissioned us to be.

3 Work in progress

Ephesians 1:15–23

'I'm on a journey.' This phrase is repeated so often today, in such different circumstances and to such different ends, that it has become something of a cliché. 'I'm on a journey' can mean 'Don't judge me for failing (or even for not trying in the first place).' It can mean 'I'm a deep, profound spiritual person—watch, look and learn.' But it can also mean 'I'm on a journey. I am moving, changing, growing, developing, but I am not there yet.'

Sometimes Christians can get anxious about this. Christ was unique. His mission was sufficient. His death was unrepeatable. His resurrection was the final word. 'It is finished' (John 19:30). God has done what he has done and all that is left for us is to say 'yes' (or perhaps 'no'). What journey is there left?

Yet these truths can mask as much as they reveal, as today's passage shows. Paul knew, above anyone else, the finality and totality of Christ's death and resurrection. He knew that no human striving could add to or detract from what God had done. But he also knew that he and his congregations were work in progress—on a journey that began with their 'yes' to Christ.

Hence he recognises and celebrates their faith and love (v. 15). He gives thanks for them (v. 16). And then he prays that they may know God better (v. 17), 'that the eyes of their heart may be enlightened' (v. 18) to know God's hope, riches and power (v. 19).

It's not that they don't know this. It is, after all, this power that raised Christ from the dead (v. 20) and appointed him head of all creation for the church (v. 22), of which the Ephesians are a part. As far as we can tell, they know all this—and yet they don't know it. They know it with their minds but not with their hearts. Or they know it with their hearts, but only in part.

As with them, so with us. No matter how long we have been a Christian, there is so much more to learn and to know; so much more of ourselves to change and be transformed (see Philippians 1:6; 2 Corinthians 3:18). It is a cliché but clichés are sometimes true. We are on a journey.

4 The sobering reality of where we start

Ephesians 2:1–10

It's an old joke and you will have heard it before.

A city dweller, on his way to another city, finds himself lost in the countryside. He stops to ask a local who is loitering on the roadside the way to his destination (there are as many different destinations as there are versions of the joke). The local does his best to help the lost soul on his way but no matter how hard he tries he can't explain how to get there. Eventually, throwing up his arms in despair, he says, 'Well, if I were you, I really wouldn't start from here.'

Ideally, we wouldn't really start from where Paul does in this rich and pungent passage, with an emphasis on sin and spiritual death. Humans are wonderful creatures—capable of enormous creativity, generosity, intelligence, kindness and love. We like to see ourselves in this light, and for good reason.

Paul knows this. Not only is he quite capable of recognising and praising human goodness, but, as a good first-century Jew, he knows that God's creation is fundamentally good, something to be celebrated.

But it is also something that needs redeeming, for humans are also capable of enormous cruelty (I call my first witness: the evening news) and, less dramatically but more pervasively, of not quite fulfilling our potential for generosity and kindness. Too often, in the paraphrased words of the General Confession, we leave undone those things which we ought to have done, and we do those things which we ought not to have done, 'and there is no health in us'.

This is why Paul starts where he does (and why he can be so unpalatable to an 'I'm OK, you're OK' culture). He recognises deep systemic problems—that we gratify our own cravings and desires and thoughts (v. 3), at the cost of others, even of ourselves. This isn't a problem you can paper over. We start from where we are.

But here is where the analogy with the joke breaks down, because the whole burden of Paul's message is we can't find our way back. Neither our own efforts nor the advice of any helpful locals is enough. We need not a map but a rescue mission, someone parachuted in to lead us bodily onwards to where we were always trying, but never succeeding, to arrive.

Thankfully, to paraphrase Paul, this is just what God has done, by raising us up and leading us home in Christ (v. 6).

5 Unity in love

Ephesians 2:11–18

One of the problems with Paul's letters is that he never rated them for subsequent readers. Life would have been so much more straightforward for Christians down the centuries had he been able to publish his Collected Letters in his twilight years, footnoting the quotations, referencing the people mentioned and writing an introduction in which he pointed out which bits of which letters he thought were particularly important, and which were more spur-of-the-moment stuff.

Size is obviously important—Romans would surely have got an A-grade from its author—but I have a sneaking suspicion that he would have rated Ephesians, and in particular today's passage, as one of his high points. Because it is in these ten or so verses that he captures the gospel with admirable conciseness.

It's all about reconciliation. Circumcised and uncircumcised, Jew and Gentile, God's chosen people and those who were seemingly not chosen by him: these two groups are brought together once and for all in the flesh of God's own son. Those markers—circumcision and law—so essential to the identity of one group (and, by implication, the other group who are left on the outside), are set aside. Now we have 'one new humanity out of the two' (v. 15).

But it's not just horizontal reconciliation or reconciliation between peoples. It's about vertical reconciliation too, between humans and God. For there is little hope of (and for) a reconciled and united humanity that remains at war with, or in exile from, its maker. So it is that Paul's talk of reconciliation between Jew and Gentile in the blood of Christ runs straight into—indeed, is rooted deep in—talk of reconciling both of them to God through the cross (v. 16). The hope of humans being at one with one another is founded on their being at one—their at-onement—with God. It's a key passage, made even more impressive by verse 18: 'through him we both have access to the Father by one Spirit', which is one of those New Testament seeds from which the doctrine of the Trinity would grow and blossom.

There's so much there and yet, at the same time, so much simplicity. If you want an answer to who God is, what he has done, what we should do, how we should live, it is in the picture of two formerly estranged parties coming together in peace and reconciliation.

6 No longer aliens

Ephesians 2:19–22

As I write, the United Nations has expressed concern about Lebanon shutting its borders to Syrian refugees. You can hardly blame Lebanon—it has absorbed a vast number of Syrians, more than a million—but it's still another agony for the victims of the Syrian civil war to endure.

Being a refugee is a profoundly distressing experience: not only physically tough but mentally and emotionally destabilising. It forces people to question what most of us take for granted. Where do I belong? What I am doing here? Who am I?

Christians both are and are not refugees. Paul here is giving his readers the good news. Once they were refugees (not a bad translation of 'foreigners and strangers' in v. 19) from God, not because of any civil war they were fleeing, but because they were, by their very nature, insurgents, rebelling against God's rule and remaining outside his redeemed covenant people

God's response to this, however, was not to obliterate them, or even to wait until they laid down their arms and came crawling back for mercy. Rather, it was to come himself into their rebel camp and invite them into his kingdom, where his own people, Israel, had been living well (more or, usually, less) for years. The borders were thrown open on the cross, and the refugees invited back to the country they had left.

That's one side of the story. However Peter writes in his first letter 'to God's elect', advising them to 'live out your time as foreigners here in reverent fear... [and], as foreigners and exiles, to abstain from sinful desires' (1 Peter 1:1, 17; 2:11). This was an identity clearly taken to heart by the early Christians, who were said to 'take their full part as citizens, but they also submit to anything and everything as if they were aliens' (*Letter to Diognetus*, ch. 5).

This was the flip side. The very fact of becoming 'fellow citizens with God's people and also members of his household' (Ephesians 2:19) meant the early Christians became strangers, to a degree, in their own cultures, worshipping a different God, living different lives, holding different values. For those of us who live in a culture that still glows with Christian history and values, this may be only a vague feeling we have (if at all). But for many around the world it is a harsh reality, and one for which we should earnestly pray.

Guidelines

Who are you? How do you see yourself? Where is your home, your identity, your security? It is sometimes said that the Holy Spirit disturbs the comfortable and comforts the disturbed. So it is here. For those of us who too easily find our security in the world—job, possessions, nationhood, ethnicity, even family—pray that we might feel more intensely Christ's claim on us, that his love and his unity may be our home. And for those many Christians elsewhere for whom the world is a threat—discriminated against at work, threatened by political regimes, persecuted by religious authorities—and who have no choice but to ground their whole security in Christ, pray they may know peace in the fullest *shalom* sense, not simply absence of war but hospitality, rest, comfort, support and love wherever on earth they find themselves.

8–14 February

1 'One'

Ephesians 4:1–16

Last week we looked at the opening two chapters of Ephesians, in which Paul flies over some of the big themes of the gospel—grace, predestination, forgiveness, redemption, reconciliation—pointing them out to his audience in his typically dense and animated style before moving on.

Chapter 3, which we have skipped over for reasons of space, interrupts the flow of his argument with an autobiographical aside followed by a heartfelt prayer for the Ephesians. Chapter 4 then begins the letter's descent, not so much leaving the features of the first half as showing what they look like from the ground—we might say, where the rubber hits the runway. Theology and ethics are not separate things in Paul's mind, nor should they be in any Christian's.

So it is that in this passage we have Paul picking up on the theme of reconciliation, about which he wrote in chapter 2, and using it to emphasise the critical importance of unity in the Christian life. Here we get one of the definitive statements of Christian monotheism and its implications: 'one body... one Spirit... one hope... one Lord... one faith... one baptism... one God and Father' (vv. 4–6).

Paul knew from his experience of other churches how divisions could creep in, and he also knew how inimical that divisiveness was to Christ's mission and message of reconciliation; hence the overpowering emphasis on making 'every effort to keep the unity of the Spirit through the bond of peace' (v. 3). Unity is not the same as uniformity. Each of us has been given talents and a calling to equip us for works of service. But those talents are for the good of each other, for the common good, rather than for our own satisfaction.

It all sounds good on paper but it is remarkably tough in life. Christians have grievous centuries of disunity behind them, and all of us are continually inclined to use our skills to build up ourselves, even when we do pay lip service to the common good.

The battle for unity is an ongoing one, which is why we need constant reminding that this isn't just an ethical nice-to-have but, as Paul outlined in chapter 2, absolutely central to who God is and what he values.

2 Honesty, creativity, generosity

Ephesians 4:17–28

Today's passage picks up on the theme of Gentiles joining with God's people that Paul emphasised in chapter 2 ('you who once were far away have been brought near', 2:13) and unpacks what that means for their everyday lives.

Paul paints a gloomy and, it must be admitted, somewhat exaggerated picture of what Gentile life in the classical world was like. It could have been more enlightened and more humane than he depicts in verses 17–19. But it could also have been as he describes it—brutal, selfish and indulgent. And if that was the way of life his Ephesian audience had been used to, it shouldn't be like that any more. They were to be made new, with a new attitude to life and, crucially, wearing a new self 'created to be like God in true righteousness and holiness' (v. 24). This is the image of God, which we were made to bear but which we repeatedly throw off or tear up. It is the 'glory of Christ, who is the image of God' as Paul puts it in 2 Corinthians 4:4. It's what we should be like, what we're not like, and what we have been given back by Christ.

What does that look like in practice? Verses 25–28 are dense with ethical commands, not of the 'do this or perish' variety, nor of the 'it would be nice if you could live this way' variety but of Paul's typical 'if you really are in Christ, then this is what follows' variety.

There's much here but I want to focus in particular on verse 28 which (I think) is one of the best sentences Paul ever wrote. He begins where all too often Christians have ended their ethical thinking: 'Don't steal.' It's good advice, which we should follow. But then he goes on to explain that 'not stealing' is not an end in itself. Ethics is more than a series of nos. Instead, we should do something useful with our own hands. The God in whose image we are made is creative. So we should be creative. His real genius is to go still further, however, and say that we must create so we may have 'something to share with those in need'. God is generous as well as creative, and if we are to put on God's self, our goal must be generosity, to give and share with others just as Christ did.

3 Mind your language

Ephesians 4:29—5:7

We know a surprising amount about the very early church, given how tiny, vulnerable and socially insignificant it was. But, of course, there is a great deal more we don't know and wish we did. We know, for example, that there was some tension between Peter and Paul, but we know hardly anything about the relationship between James and Paul. Many suspect there was even more tension here, James being the leader of the more conservative, law-focused Jerusalem church.

But even if that were so, there are still conspicuous similarities between, for example, what James wrote in his one surviving letter about speech and what Paul says here. James emphasised how even though the tongue was a small part of the body, it could make great boasts, sparking raging fires and corrupting lives. 'Those who consider themselves religious and yet do not keep a tight rein on their tongues deceive themselves, and their religion is worthless' (James 1:26).

That is pretty much Paul's point of view also. You may call yourself a follower of Christ, yet if your speech is unwholesome, obscene, foolish, coarse, empty or, worse still, marked by bitterness, rage, slander and malice you are betraying your real self. Use the tongue instead for unity (that theme again), to build one another up—for compassion, forgiveness, love—and to give thanks to God.

Now we must be slightly careful here. It is easy to go beyond what Paul is advocating to full-scale joylessness, in which the earnest Christian avoids not only foolishness but also fun. The caricature of the dour, humourless, puritanical Christian, avoiding all talk that might make you smile, is, alas, not without foundation. Paul is not, it must be acknowledged, big on humour but his repeated emphasis on joy reminds us that the solemn, gloomy caricature of him is unlikely to be right.

The key here, as so often in this letter, is unity. Spiteful talk—destructive, slanderous, base, malicious—hurts people, destroys relationships, divides communities and dishonours God. Kind, compassionate, forgiving talk does the opposite. We should endeavour to check what we say and use our words to build relationships rather than destroy them.

4 Information, knowledge, wisdom

Ephesians 5:8–20

There's an awful lot of information in the world today. We are, we are told, living in the information age in which information technology shapes pretty much everything we do, from the computer on which I am writing this to the press that eventually prints it.

But information itself is pretty worthless unless formed into knowledge, and knowledge itself is vulnerable and impoverished unless formed into wisdom. We have a habit, as the poet T.S. Eliot once noted (in 'The Rock'), of losing wisdom in knowledge and knowledge in information.

Paul, like so many other biblical writers, wants us to live wisely. That means knowing what God's will is and shaping our thoughts, words and deeds accordingly. The wise life seeks to know God in the fullest way possible. (Note again, by the way, the early trinitarian formula in vv. 18–20: 'be filled with the Spirit… always giving thanks to God the Father… in the name of our Lord Jesus Christ'.) The wise life is a thankful life, grateful to God for what we have received and what he has done.

Above all, using the metaphor that Paul dwells on in this passage, it is a life lived in the light. Sometimes metaphors lose their edge over the centuries (there are plenty of Paul's referring to the law courts or the marketplace that require explanation today), but the metaphor of light does not.

In the darkness we fumble, stub toes, walk into doors, fall down stairs, hurt ourselves. We go slowly, hesitantly, fearfully. In the light, we know ourselves and our environment. We understand where we are and where we are going. We have (a measure of) control over our lives, which allows us to shape who we are.

This is what the light of Christ affords us. Paul mixes his metaphors dreadfully when he talks, in verse 9, about 'the fruit of the light' (he was an inveterate metaphor-mixer) but we understand him nonetheless. The wise life is lived in the light of Christ, which produces goodness, righteousness and truth that is good to taste and beneficial to all.

That is the wisdom we should seek, even as we chart the ever-deepening waters of the information age.

5 Living well together

Ephesians 5:21—6:9

Of all the passages in Ephesians, this one is most likely to be read nervously by the 21st-century Western Christian. All Paul's talk of slaves and submission strikes us as very backward, very primitive; an example of the kind of hierarchy and oppression from which we liberal moderns have, thankfully, been freed.

Of course, it would be easy to draw on this passage—or, more precisely, single phrases and verses from it—to justify the worst excesses of exploitation and power play. Many Christians have. 'Wives, submit to your own husbands… Children, obey your parents… Slaves, obey your earthly masters' (5:25; 6:1, 5): taken like that it sounds like a dictator's charter.

But verses can be taken out of context to prove anything. Thus, in place of these verses we might prefer 'Submit to one another… husbands ought to love their wives as their own bodies… Fathers, do not exasperate your children… [masters] do not threaten [your slaves]' (5:21, 28; 6:4, 9): that all sounds very different.

The truth is these ethical commands, like those preceding them, were never intended to act like a stand-alone set of commandments, independent of everything else Paul wrote. It is when we read them plucked out of Paul's wider teaching that we are liable to get them wrong, finding in them the liberal attitudes of our culture or the authoritarian attitudes of our heart.

Once again, Paul is bringing us down to earthy reality from the high-flying theology of the first half of the letter, in particular his theology of unity in love. Yes, people are different. Everyone has different gifts and roles and functions in society, and yes they are all challenging. Seeing a wife treat her husband as if he had no authority is as uncomfortable as watching a husband talk to his wife as if she were unloved and unappreciated; ditto children disrespecting their parents, or parents bullying their children.

The issue with slaves is more complicated, hinging greatly on the vexed question of what slavery was then. Suffice it to say, it was precisely that emphasis on unity in love that eventually saw the Christian West undermine and then abolish the idea of slavery.

Here especially in Ephesians we see how important it is to read Paul's theology into his ethics, and his ethics from his theology.

6 The armour of God

Ephesians 6:10–24

Our last passage from Ephesians is perhaps the letter's best known. Beloved by Sunday schools the world over, it is remarkable if for no other reason than it sees Paul stick with a single metaphor for seven whole verses without lurching off in different metaphorical directions as the ideas take him.

How do you get people to remember and appreciate and live the virtues of the gospel—truth, righteousness, readiness, peace and faith? Why not do essentially what the cross itself does and turn a device of harm, aggression and pain into one of peace?

Just as Christ took the cross and by conquering it showed that Caesar no longer ruled through it, so Paul here takes military hardware, of the kind worn by those who crucified his Lord, and turns it into armour of the gospel: 'the belt of truth… the breastplate of righteousness… the shield of faith… the helmet of salvation' (vv. 14–17). In doing so he emphasises his main point in this concluding passage, namely that the Christian fight is not against 'flesh and blood' (v. 12) but something much more profound (and powerful). Christians are not going to win anything through military intervention, or an election—which is not to say that armed conflict and political processes are irrelevant.

Rather, the fight is 'against the rulers… the authorities… the powers… the spiritual forces' (v. 12). It is far from clear how we should interpret this, and Christians have differed greatly over the centuries, from seeing the fight as basically the same as an earthly battle, only taking place somewhere in the sky, all the way to seeing it as an intellectual fight, one in which the right ideas are pitted against the wrong ones. However we interpret Paul here (and elsewhere), though, it is clear that the canvas on which he paints is a vast, mysterious and elusive one.

But it is not one that should cause us to despair. We have been equipped for the fight and, just as long as we remember that the victor has gone before his army, and the victory he has won is one of unity in love, then we, like Paul, may go on, as he says twice near the end, making known the mystery of the gospel 'fearlessly' (vv. 19, 20).

Guidelines

'What so-and-so did as a banker/politician/journalist/police officer [insert your role of choice here[was technically perfectly legal.' It's a defence we have heard quite a lot over recent years. And it never washes. The response comes straight back, 'Yes, but it wasn't moral.'

It's a telling riposte, because it reveals what really matters to us. Picking up and paraphrasing what we read in Ephesians this week, 'not stealing' is not enough. The good life is not one that simply avoids breaking the law. It is also creative and generous.

Or, again, having lots of information at your fingertips is not enough. Nor even is knowing lots of stuff. The good life is not the clever life but the wise life. Or, once again, not being spiteful about others is not enough. The good life is one where we speak well of, build up, support, forgive and love one another in what we say.

So perhaps we can be guided by these examples. How can we be creative and generous in our relationships with one another? How can we be wise in our decisions? How can we edify those with whom we speak?

Above all, can we see Christ himself in the faces of those we interact with, no matter how blurred that image may in fact be? How then might we treat those people? Pray for the strength and resolve to do this, and for forgiveness when we inevitably fail!

FURTHER READING

Tom Wright, *Paul for Everyone: The prison letters—Ephesians, Philippians, Colossians and Philemon* (SPCK, 2002).

John Stott, *The Message of Ephesians: God's new society* (*The Bible Speaks Today*) (IVP, 1991).

F.F. Bruce, *The Epistle to the Ephesians: A verse-by-verse exposition* (Kindle: Robert Frederick, 2012).

Luke 1—4

Luke claims he is writing his Gospel with considerable care. There are at least three stages involved in his presentation. There is his own written 'orderly account' (1:3), which is the result of his careful investigation and his intention to help Theophilus know the truth; prior to this are the many other accounts of 'the events that have been fulfilled among us' (1:1)—we do not know whether they were written or oral. Preceding these was the oral *tradition* 'handed on to us' by those who had two necessary qualifications: they were 'eyewitnesses' and 'servants of the word' (1:2). Not all eyewitnesses were going to offer a trustworthy account. There were some who could be persuaded to give false witness! Every word mentioned here has been meticulously examined by scholars but what we can conclude is this. Firstly there was much being said and written about Jesus in the first decades following his death. Clearly, for this to have happened, he must have generated a lot of interest and there were many available sources from which to glean information. Secondly there was the intention to ensure that what was presented was reliable and valid. Thirdly Luke felt there was the need for his own presentation to help Theophilus.

We start with the material leading up to the birth of Jesus, before moving to the beginnings of Jesus' public ministry. (An observant reader will notice that Luke 2 receives scant comment. This is because it was dealt with in the previous issue of *Guidelines*, as part of the Christmas material.) Luke provides us with an account of Jesus' own understanding of his mission by allowing us to listen in on his sermon in Nazareth. But first we are helped to recognise who Jesus really is, through his baptism, his genealogy and his temptations. We are then given specific examples of how Jesus went about fulfilling his mission in the synagogues, in people's homes and outdoors. Interwoven with all of this are indications of his growing popularity and the opposition he was generating.

Quotations are taken from the New Revised Standard Version.

1 An imposing entrance

Luke 1:1–4

These verses are like an imposing classical entrance to a stately home. Luke's style is rich and well proportioned. To what extent this reflects his natural ability as a writer, his reverence for the story he is going to unfold or his desire to appeal to the 'most excellent Theophilus' (v. 3), we can only speculate. Indeed, who Theophilus is we can, unfortunately, only guess. Is this his patron's proper name? Is it a pseudonym, and if so was it used to protect his identity or was Luke simply being winsome—for it means 'lover of God'? Or should it be understood as referring to a community which is here personified?

Already we see that in spite of its apparent clarity, this passage raises many fascinating issues, which are still largely unanswered. What we can probably discern are the following.

Producing accounts of the life of Jesus (for that is what 'an account of the events' must refer to in view of what follows) has clearly become an important business, as 'many have undertaken' it (v. 1). This seems to have been a community activity, because the events were 'fulfilled [or 'surely believed', KJV]) among us' (v. 1) and they were 'handed on to us' (v. 2). This raises the question as to how many such accounts Luke knew about. Was it only Matthew and Mark and maybe John? This hardly seems enough to satisfy the 'many'. We know of several 'apocryphal Gospels' but these are normally dated much later than Luke's. So how much knowledge and memory of Jesus are we lacking?

If Luke is to be accepted, we have not missed very much, for he is intent on thoroughly researching and evaluating the available sources (he 'investigated everything carefully from the beginning': v. 3, CEB). 'Beginning' could mean the start of the life of Jesus or the earliest available resources, right back to the 'eyewitnesses and servants of the word' (v. 2). Certainly Luke includes more about the birth of Jesus and his connections with John the Baptist than the writers of the other Gospels we have. What Luke offers, then, is an 'orderly account' (v. 3). This might suggest chronological order, or the thoroughness with which historical and geographical locations are provided (for example, 1:5; 2:1–4, 39–40), or the overall structure of the book.

2 An amazing birth

Luke 1:57–66

It sounds prosaic: 'Now the time came for Elizabeth to have her baby, and she bore a son' (v. 57). There was roughly a 50 per cent chance it would be a son; billions of women have done the same! So what?

Everyone around her knew the answer to that question—or part of it! 'The Lord had shown his great mercy to her, and they rejoiced with her' (v. 58). The gospel is beginning to emerge. To start with this baby is special because of the age of the parents, but the baby is also righting a perceived wrong: how come such godly people had been deprived by God of a child (see 1:5–7)? This and similar questions worry believers, and rightly so. Even in this birth there is a sign of God moving to right the world, to establish his justice for people to see. So the people recognise this act of mercy, that is, redemption.

The rejoicing of Elizabeth's neighbours and relatives is highly instructive as well as being a natural response to a family celebrating a new baby. In Luke's Gospel rejoicing is a theological response (see 1:14; 2:10–14; 10:17, 21; 15:7, 9, 22–24). Whether they know it or not, they are joining in with the angelic hosts. Rejoicing is our response to seeing and benefiting from the gracious acts of God. In expressing their joy, the people are also fulfilling the angel's prophecy in 1:14.

However, the answer to 'So what?' is more profound. The child is not to be named after his father, Zechariah, as was the very strong custom with a first son, but given a new name, John. John means 'God is gracious'. This strange name, given by divine command of course, itself indicates the beginning of a new era. Once this name is actualised, Zechariah (himself named after a significant Old Testament prophet) has his speech restored (v. 64)—another indication of God's powerful presence in this birth.

As described in verses 65–66, the events caused 'fear', were 'talked about throughout the entire hill country of Judea' and were 'pondered', underlining people's instinctive recognition of a momentous, divine event in this birth.

3 Released to praise

Luke 1:67–80

Zechariah's reported response on the restoration of his speech is to begin 'praising God' (1:64). All he has longed to express over these nine months rushes out in joyful praise. This burst of praise is followed by Zechariah's prophetic speech, which we read today.

Zechariah proclaims, 'He has raised up a mighty Saviour for us' (v. 69). At first reading, given the context of the birth of John the Baptist, it is natural to read this 'Saviour' as referring to John. Here is a proud father attributing this highest of all titles to his son, whose birth was announced in advance by an angel, whose conception was little short of miraculous and whose gestation was marked by the imposition of speechlessness on his father. This interpretation seems even more natural given the fact that Jesus' birth is still awaited.

For us as Christian readers, though, it appears obvious that Zechariah is referring proleptically to Jesus—who the angels make clear is the Saviour (see 2:11). How can we decide which is correct?

In verse 76, Zechariah's proclamation takes a different turn. The address is now in the second person singular: 'And you, child...' This underlines the significance of this new beginning. Here John is described as 'the prophet of the Most High'. Again, as Christian readers we are likely to understand this as an indication of the forerunning role of John the Baptist in announcing the coming of the Saviour–Messiah. But 'the prophet of the Most High' could itself be a messianic title.

Luke goes on to make this forerunner function clear (see 3:1–17), yet the prophesying of John's role in Luke 1:76–79 is compatible with a messianic calling. Perhaps we can recognise in Zechariah's prophecy the aspirations for John that led many to wonder if John was himself the Messiah.

4 Clarifying John's role

Luke 3:1–14

John the Baptist continued to be significant long after his death and into the early church period. We get a glimpse of this in Acts 19:1–7, where we meet some 'believers' who had been baptised 'into John's baptism' (19:2–3).

Given this, it is not surprising that Luke takes time to describe and elucidate John's mission. All four Gospel writers quote from Isaiah 40:3–5, but Luke quotes the most and ends with 'all flesh shall see the salvation of God' (v. 6), which relates to his understanding of the gospel. Luke contextualises John's appearance in a fascinating way. First, as with his account of the birth of Jesus, he gives the political context, naming Tiberias as emperor and then the local rulers, Pilate, Herod, Philip and Lysanias. Then (and this is lacking in the birth narrative) he names the current high priests. We now start to see that Luke is outlining not so much Roman history (as he did in the birth account) as prophetic history, because this historical context is followed by 'the word of God came to John' (v. 2). So John, though not presented as the Messiah, is clearly shown to be following in the prophetic tradition. His role is delineated as 'proclaiming a baptism of repentance for the forgiveness of sins' (v. 3). In other words, he is seeking to prepare people for the Messiah's coming.

Three types of people are indicated. First the Jewish crowd, who can claim, 'We have Abraham as our ancestor' (v. 8), then tax collectors, who were on the margins of Jewish society, and finally Roman soldiers. This movement from the centre outwards is typical of Luke's vision (compare 'in Jerusalem… to the ends of the earth' from Acts 1:8), but respects the historical evidence too; it is orderly and accurate.

Each of these three cameos consists of two parts: first the description of the group with an indication that they asked John's view, then secondly an appropriate response for each group. Repentance is seen here not simply as a change of mind, still less just feeling sorry, but in terms of what appropriate behaviour looks like (see also Luke 19:1–10). Note that John does not ask either tax collectors or soldiers to give up their occupations, but simply to carry out their tasks in a peaceful and honest manner.

5 The end of the beginning

Luke 3:15–20

What is striking in the previous episode is how little attention is given to the act of baptism. The focus is on the necessary behaviour of the people being baptised, not the act of the baptiser. Also, the *voice* crying in the wilderness seems far more important than the person himself; Luke does not pause to give us a description of John's appearance—fascinating as that seems to have been (compare Matthew 3:4; Mark 1:6). At the same time, Luke has created a sense of growing response to the baptiser through descriptions such as 'He went into all the region'—not simply 'the region' (v. 3); 'the crowds that came out to be baptised by him' (v. 7)—not just 'the crowd'; and 'Even tax collectors…' (v. 12)—not simply 'tax collectors'. All this builds to a height in his comment, 'The people were filled with expectation, and all were questioning in their hearts' (v. 15). The growing and ever more far-reaching response is now revealed as a messianic expectation for John the Baptist.

It is left to John to dismiss this powerful interest in him. His baptism is only with water. There is one coming with the Holy Spirit and fire. John certainly seems to view this as the fire of judgement or, more accurately, refinement, as verse 17's metaphor of wheat and chaff indicates. However, it is not about refining individuals so they are fit for God's kingdom (as in 1 Peter 1:7) but refining the nation—destroying with 'unquenchable fire' (v. 17) those who are corrupt. It is noteworthy that Luke leaves us a report of John's words here, even though Jesus is going to act very differently (see 4:16–30).

What is even more noteworthy is that Luke ends this section with effectively the end of John's mission. John does not stand around to usher in the Messiah's ministry. Rather he is described in verses 19–20 as being arrested and imprisoned by Herod. The way this is presented suggests that Herod is the evil power in control. Yet, as this is the fate for true prophets, Luke is also indicating and affirming John's prophetic role, while demarcating it from any messianic pretentions. There is more to come about John (see 7:18–35).

6 Jesus' baptism

Luke 3:21–22

In Acts, baptism is a very significant feature, marking out the transition from either Jewish faith or paganism into Christian salvation and membership of the Christian community (see, for example, Acts 2:37–42; 10:44–48). It is done in the name of Jesus and often associated with the giving of God's Spirit. Here Luke compresses the account of Jesus' baptism. He does not indicate that it was administered by John the Baptist and, in the light of verse 20, this could be understood to imply it wasn't, for John the Baptist had been imprisoned by Herod. (Compare John 4:2, which shows that to say someone was baptised by Jesus did not have to mean Jesus physically performed the act—rather that it was under his authority; presumably the same may have been true of 'John's baptism'.)

Is Luke intending, with this very short account, to diminish the significance of John the Baptist? In view of Luke 7:18–35, as well as the details of John's birth and Zechariah's eulogistic prophecy, this is highly unlikely. So what is going on here?

What is being indicated is the proper order of things (see Luke 1:3), as pointed to by Jesus in 7:28. John is the greatest of those 'born of women', but membership of the kingdom of God is in a higher category (compare Acts 19:1–7). So it is significant that Luke concludes his account of John's work with the words, 'Now when all the people were baptised, and when Jesus also had been baptised...' (v. 21). It is clearly not the case that *all* the people had been baptised; rather, this is an indication of the fulfilment of time. The era of John's baptism, preparing the way for Jesus, has now been completed. Being baptised by John or by one of his disciples has no more theological and salvific value now that Jesus has been baptised.

In spite of the brevity of Luke's account, he adds two things to all the others. The first is that the heavens opened as Jesus was praying. Prayer is one topic that Luke emphasises more than the other Gospels. The second feature is Luke's description of the descent of the Holy Spirit 'in bodily form like a dove' (v. 22). Although the Gospels are unanimous in describing the coming of the Spirit on Jesus as like a dove, Luke stresses that this indicates only the form, not the reality of the Spirit.

Guidelines

Luke's Gospel provides us with much special material about the conception and birth of both Jesus and John. Reread this material and select one passage (perhaps your favourite). Then spend time engaging with it in meditation and prayer. Does this exercise suggest anything about your own spiritual preferences? Does it indicate any sense of God's further calling on your life?

Luke claims to write an 'orderly account'. When you are reading a biography or an autobiography how important is chronological awareness? How much do you like interests and themes, or indeed sets of relationships, to be followed through? As you read Luke's account, what do you discern he is trying to do? What does the text suggest 'orderly' means? How important is chronology in depictions of the life of Jesus, and how important is it to follow through on issues like miracles, parables or the kingdom of God?

22–28 February

1 How it all began

Luke 3:23–38

When Luke said he was writing 'an orderly account' (1:1) what exactly did he mean? We have already considered this question, and we do so again. Here we have Luke's genealogy of Jesus. Inevitably this invites comparison with Matthew's version (Matthew 1:1–17). Matthew begins his Gospel with the genealogy—which seems to make better sense if we want 'orderly' to mean 'in historical order'. Luke places his version immediately prior to the temptation of Jesus and the start of Jesus' ministry. Indeed Luke makes this structural point very clear:

'Jesus was about thirty years old when he began his work' (v. 23).

Another difference is that Matthew starts at the beginning (with Abraham) and moves forward to the parents of Jesus. Luke works backwards from Jesus to his origins. He goes further back than Matthew too, beyond Abraham, right the way back to Adam, and by implication beyond him—for Adam is the 'son of God' (v. 38). Matthew follows what appears to be the Hebrew norm in setting out genealogies. For instance 1 Chronicles 1 begins with Adam, moves through to Abraham then eventually reaches the twelve sons or tribes of Israel (see 1 Chronicles 1:1—2:2). In Genesis the same dynamic is followed (see, for example, Genesis 5:1–22; 10:1–32).

What Luke seems to be doing is making a theological rather than a historical point. Jesus, like Adam, is God's son. That is what God declared at his baptism. This is what the temptations are going to put to the test. However, unlike Adam, Jesus did not fail. He remains the 'son of God'. Indeed this is what the earlier chapters have also been establishing. When Gabriel announced to Mary that she would conceive as the Holy Spirit came upon her and the power of the Most High overshadowed her (using Hebrew parallelism to indicate the same reality with two different sets of words), he rounded off his declaration with the words 'he will be called Son of God' (1:35).

Luke, then, is indicating the theological reality of Jesus rather than simply his historical antecedents. Things are not exactly what they seem. Jesus 'was the son (as was thought) of Joseph son of Heli' (v. 23), yet his birth did not begin with his human ancestors but with God.

2 Ifs and no buts

Luke 4:1–8

At the heart of the first temptation, to turn stones into bread, is the critical issue of the nature of sonship: 'If you are the Son of God...' (v. 3). Does privilege inevitably lead to the abuse of power for one's own benefits? But for Jesus the temptation goes even deeper. At the heart of sonship is obedience to every word that comes from God (see Matthew 4:4). Yet even more important than obedience is the inherent trust that it requires. The verse that Jesus quotes, Deuteronomy 8:3, is part of the story of God feeding Israel with manna in the wilderness, doing a completely new thing to save his people.

It is one thing to be confronted by the devil in conversation, as described in the first temptation. It is quite another to seem as though you are in the devil's power. 'Then the devil led him up' (v. 5) suggests that Jesus was apparently in Satan's control.

Jesus must have had a powerful longing for God's rule to be restored to all the kingdoms of the world, and the offer of an opportunity to take control of them taps into that desire. But what this temptation searches out at the deepest level is whether Jesus really wants God's kingdom and the blessings for all the earth for God's sake, or whether he wants to be at the heart of bringing this about for his own sake.

Here too is a second 'if': 'If you, then, will worship me…' (v. 7). Jesus' refusal to accept the devil's offer indicates that he has no personal ego agenda. All must be, and is, completely surrendered to God. Jesus is absolutely committed to the service and worship of God.

But what are we to make of the devil's claim that all the glory and authority of all the kingdoms has been given over to him and he can distribute it as he chooses (v. 6)? The use of the passive, as in 'has been given', is often in scripture understood as a reverential way to indicate divine activity (Luke 6:37; 11:9; 12:2; 14:14, to offer a very few examples). It seems to suggest, at least, that Satan is not the supreme authority, even when he appears to act as such. So in making the condition for his 'generous offer' that Jesus must worship him, there is a very serious misdirection. Ultimate allegiance can and should only be given to the ultimate authority.

3 Learning to trust

Luke 4:9–13

If Jesus wants to stubbornly insist that he will only worship God, then the devil will take him to the centre of that worship—the temple in Jerusalem. If Jesus wants to defend himself by quoting scripture, then the devil can do the same.

The devil was too astute to remind Jesus he was the Son of God when he wanted Jesus to pledge himself to worship Satan! But now he plays this card again. Now the temptation is not to doubt God's ability to provide (as in 4:3), but the converse: if you really trust God, as you say you do, then prove it by throwing yourself down from the great height of the temple pinnacle. If you don't accept this dare then you reveal your lack of trust in God. At least this is the implication. Both the scriptural quotations endorse this understanding.

Jesus perceives, however, that seeking to establish beyond doubt that God will protect him when he undertakes something foolhardy and attention-seeking is itself a form of doubt. By performing such a feat, with its anticipated miraculous outcome, he would not only be drawing attention to himself; he would be seeking to manipulate God's power. To do so, therefore, would be to test God. At the heart of such an act would be doubt not trust, not submission but manipulation.

This temptation in more subtle forms would track Jesus through his ministry. He was not free to do miraculous things to prove he was who he said he was (Luke 4:23; John 6:30); he would not use his powers to impose his will on people (Luke 9:51–56); he could not accept the kingship the crowds wanted to thrust on him (John 6:15); and his pathway was not one of self-aggrandisement but of suffering and total surrender to the Father's will (Luke 9:18–22; 22:39–44).

It is therefore no relief when Luke adds that the devil departed from him; rather, the tone is ominous. Yes, Jesus had resisted every test, but the devil would return at 'an opportune time' (v. 13).

4 The message gets out

Luke 4:14–15

The Holy Spirit (along with prayer, joy, riches and women) receives more attention in Luke than in the other synoptic Gospels. Here Jesus is 'filled with the power of the Spirit' (v. 14); in 4:1 he was 'full of the Holy Spirit'. It was Elizabeth, 'filled with the Holy Spirit', who recognised the nature of the child Mary had conceived (1:39–43). It would be when the early church was filled with the Spirit that the mission of Jesus would continue on earth following his ascension. The people of Nazareth, his home town, may have understood Jesus simply as a child prodigy, with a precocious wisdom and knowledge of God (see 2:40, 52). For Luke, though, this is not adequate. All Jesus is and does is dependent on the Holy Spirit. His work is God's work; through all he says and does, God is at work.

There are two points worth reflecting on in the light of this. First, being filled with the Spirit in itself does not make Jesus unique. Of course, we know he was also conceived of the Holy Spirit (1:35), and of no one else did an angel announce, 'A Saviour who is Christ the Lord'! So Luke made it absolutely clear to his readers that Jesus was unique, as indeed the description at his baptism implies (3:22). Nevertheless, the filling with the Spirit, while being necessary, is not sufficient for this understanding. Being filled with the Spirit identifies us with Jesus and Jesus with God, but is a potentiality of being human.

Secondly Luke is assuring us that the temptations, severe and penetrating as they were, have not diminished the presence of God in Jesus in any way. Jesus is not wounded or drained by his satanic testings. Indeed the phrase 'filled with the *power* of the Spirit' (my emphasis) probably indicates the opposite. Having being through this fiery ordeal, Jesus is now even more equipped for his mission.

Luke's order is interesting too. He tells us that reports about Jesus were spreading through Galilee before he indicates that Jesus began to teach in the synagogues. It would appear more 'orderly' to reverse this sequence. Is it simply that he wants to make a link to the next section, with his reference to synagogues? Or is Luke indicating that people were being divinely prepared to receive Jesus' message?

5 Jesus' mission

Luke 4:16–21

This passage is critical for understanding Jesus' ministry. In these verses he links his own mission to the Old Testament and by so doing makes significant claims for himself.

There has been considerable scholarly discussion about several aspects of this passage. To start with, was there some kind of lectionary in place this early on in the life of the synagogues, or was Jesus free to select this passage, Isaiah 61:1–2?

Secondly, it was normal for any adult male to read the scriptures (in Hebrew) and then comment in Aramaic—the popular language. However, Luke seems to be following the Greek translation of Isaiah (the Septuagint). In one sense this is not surprising in that Luke was writing in Greek. But there are some significant differences. The way the original Hebrew text is written suggests there are three points being made twice each (parallelism): good news to the oppressed/broken-hearted; release to captives/prisoners; proclamation of the year of the Lord's favour (the parallel here being the rather different day of God's vengeance). The Greek in Luke 4 reads as if there are five distinct, although associated, activities.

Thirdly, there is discussion as to how much the year of jubilee provides the background for Isaiah 61 and also Luke 4. The instructions for this year are in Leviticus 25:8–55. The extent to which this background should be taken into account affects the way this passage is interpreted. Some scholars see it as primarily a political text implying that the end of the exile is to be accomplished: Israel will be released from her occupiers. Others see it as a social text: the poor in the land will have their true place restored. Others emphasise the fact that Jesus omitted the line from Isaiah about 'the day of vengeance of our God' (Isaiah 61:2) and so focus on the peace and reconciliation component of Jesus' message. I suggest that the best commentary on these verses, and hence the mission of Jesus, is the next 20 chapters, in which Luke goes on to tell us about Jesus' ministry!

It is important to note that Jesus claims to fulfil this prophetic text. The reference to the Spirit of the Lord should be read in the light of Jesus' baptism (3:21–22) but not only this, as Luke makes many more references to the Spirit and Jesus.

6 Jesus' rejection

Luke 4:22–30

Whether Jesus' first hearers thought he himself was claiming to fulfil the role described by Isaiah or were more excited by the sense that God was about to act to release them (from whatever they had in mind) is not clear. Perhaps it was the growing sense that Jesus was claiming this role for himself which contributed to their alienation from him.

Certainly this alienation takes place with apparent rapidity. The saying 'no prophet is accepted in the prophet's home town' (v. 24) makes good sense in this context. In other words, Jesus is stating that he is 'the prophet', the one to which this passage is referring. After all it does use first-person language: 'The Spirit of the Lord is upon *me*... anointed *me*... sent *me*' (v. 18, my emphasis).

However, what seem to truly anger the hearers are the stories Jesus uses to indicate that God's gracious acts of deliverance (from death) and healing (from leprosy) were being offered not to those in Israel but to foreigners. This, of course, relates to the omission of the line about 'the day of vengeance of our God'. Jesus did not share the contemporary view that deliverance for one set of people must entail the destruction of another set. Within the rest of Isaiah 61 there are also lines that can be read as emphasising the universal impact of God's deliverance, not least the final verse: 'For as the earth brings forth its shoots, and as a garden causes what is sown in it to spring up, so the Lord God will cause righteousness and praise to spring up before all the nations' (Isaiah 61:11).

This universal ethos was vital for Luke's larger purposes, as unpacked in Acts. It is, however, also mirrored in Jesus' teaching on the need to 'Love your enemies' (Luke 6:27–36)—most naturally understood as the Roman occupiers and the Samaritans—as well as in the healing of the Roman centurion's slave in Luke 7:1–10.

Finally we can note that the attempt to kill Jesus (as a false prophet?) in Luke 4:28–30 is a foretaste of what will happen to Jesus later in Jerusalem. What happened in his own town will then happen in his own country. In the end he will once more pass 'through the midst of them' and go on his way to universal mission (24:50–51).

Guidelines

How important is it to your understanding of Jesus that we are given in the Gospels an account of his temptations? (See Hebrews 2:17–18; 4:14–16.)

These notes emphasise the ways in which the temptations relate to Jesus' sense of calling to be 'God's Son'. Do you find this helpful or do you prefer to see how they can be applied to our normal human situations? If so, to what do they relate? Do you think they connect with politicians' tendencies to misuse or abuse power to their own advantage (turning stone to bread), or to their motivation to serve others (rule their 'world' in a better way), which is easily distorted (worship me)? Is it only politicians who face these temptations? Pray for all who may be subject to them.

There seems to be no indication here that Jesus experienced sexual temptations. Does that matter to you? Do you think there are pointers elsewhere in the Gospels that this was ever an issue for Jesus? Are there other fundamental aspects of our human experience of temptations that are not covered either here or elsewhere in the Gospels?

Pray for yourself and others you know who may be struggling with specific temptations.

1 What did Jesus do?

Luke 4:31–37

As we read these verses immediately after the description of what took place at the synagogue in Nazareth and its aftermath, it is natural for us to understand this event in Capernaum as taking place after the sermon in Nazareth and the attempt on Jesus' life. That may be correct. However, in the light of 4:23, where Jesus expects the people of Nazareth to say, 'Do here… the things that we have heard you did at Capernaum'), perhaps Luke is showing us what might have been in the people's minds, to make such a challenge likely.

We have noted that by an 'orderly account' Luke may not simply mean chronological order. In this case, then, when he reports Jesus' words about Capernaum, he decides not to interrupt the flow of the Nazareth narrative to explain what has taken place in Capernaum. Rather, he completes the account of the Nazareth synagogue in an orderly fashion. In doing so, he keeps us guessing and so heightens our interest in what went on in Capernaum. If this is a deliberate strategy, then it also has dramatic value.

Jesus teaches in Capernaum too. (From the Nazareth events, we know the kinds of things he would say.) People are 'astounded' at his authority (v. 32) (or, indeed, his claim to be authorised by God). A demonised man reacts, speaking in the voice of the demons (note the 'us', although Luke describes him as having 'the spirit of *an* unclean demon' (v. 33, my emphasis)). The demons are afraid they will be destroyed and the man or the spirit of the demon displays his knowledge of Jesus as 'the Holy One of God' (v. 34—note the singular 'I know'). To know someone's name was to claim authority over them.

Jesus then exercises his divine authority, commanding the demon (singular again) to be silent and then to leave the man (v. 35). The man is thrown to the ground, and it is perceived by the people that 'unclean spirits' (plural) have left him (v. 36). As a result reports about Jesus begin to circulate.

In spite of the observation that the man was not harmed, the focus is not on the man or his deliverance, but on the demonstration of the authority of Jesus. Normally, Luke shows concern for the sick person, so this attention on authority rather than the person who has been delivered is important. Like Moses and Aaron before Pharaoh, Jesus has proved that he has such authority.

2 The mother-in-law

Luke 4:38–44

In the healing of Simon Peter's mother-in-law, we may get a glimpse of Doctor Luke's special interests. He describes the illness precisely—she has a 'high fever' (v. 38); Mark 1:30 simply mentions a fever. However,

Jesus treats this physical illness in a similar way to the so-called demon possession. He 'rebuked' the fever (v. 39); Luke uses the same word for 'rebuked' here as he did with the demon-possessed man. Jesus does not rebuke the mother-in-law, whereas the Greek in the account of the demon-possessed man is ambivalent: he might be rebuking the man or the demon. The details are also more intimate: 'he stood over her... Immediately she got up' (v. 39).

Once the Sabbath was over ('as the sun was setting...' (v. 40)) and people were free to carry 'burdens', they brought the sick. Jesus 'laid his hands on each of them' (v. 40), rather than rebuking the illnesses or the sick people, although he still 'rebuked' the demons and silenced them (v. 41). Their utterances—'You are the Son of God!'—are even more telling than those of the unclean spirit in 4:34. So, having provided us with two specific accounts of deliverance and healing, Luke now fills in the gaps, allowing us to build up a broader picture of Jesus' activities in Capernaum.

At daybreak, Jesus seeks solitude, but is not allowed it for long. Understandably those who are sick or who have sick relatives are clamouring for help. In contrast to Nazareth where they wanted to kill Jesus, the crowds try to insist he stays with them. But he has to move on, to 'proclaim the good news of the kingdom of God' (v. 43). Interestingly he adds, 'for I was sent for this purpose'. This kind of language recalls much in the Gospel of John (for example, 3:16; 10:36). We should also read the passive voice as meaning 'God has sent me.' Not only do the demons know who Jesus is; he is well aware himself!

3 The sinner

Luke 5:1–11

We've already come across Simon Peter's mother-in-law; now we see, for the first time, an encounter between Jesus and the man himself. Again, this suggests that Luke may not be giving us the events in chronological order.

This passage gives us an apparently very different account of the call of Simon Peter to be a disciple of Jesus from those in the other Gospels.

Mark and Matthew recount that Jesus calls two pairs of brothers by the Lake of Galilee in the briefest of terms (see Mark 1:16–20; Matthew 4:18–22), while John's sequence of events is very different (John 1:35–42). We can accept that the Gospel accounts are rather unreliable and contradictory, while acknowledging that Jesus did have a group of disciples who must have joined him at some point in some way, or we can explore whether these accounts may be intended to fit together.

Although the latter approach is often dismissed as an attempt to synthesise completely incompatible narratives, before we reject this approach out of hand there are some details in the Luke passage which may challenge us to think differently. First, while all the focus is on Simon Peter, the story begins with '[Jesus] saw *two* boats…' (v. 2, my emphasis). James and John are not named here but are drawn into the flow of events later (v. 10) because of the extremely large catch of fish. There is nothing s aid about their invitation to follow Jesus but, as we shall see, clearly they do! So it makes perfect sense to read this story as Luke filling out the details of how the call of Simon Peter happened. He is going to be a key player for Luke, especially in Acts.

The second point to note is that although the boat is described as belonging to Simon Peter, it is clear that he is not manning it alone. Although he says, '*I* will let down the nets' (v. 5), verses 6–7 repeatedly refer to 'they, 'their' and 'them'. Clearly there are others in the boat. Also there is another boat (v. 7), belonging to their 'partners' who we discover later are James and John (v. 10). Finally, although Jesus addresses Simon Peter with the words 'you [singular] will be catching people', verse 11 tells us 'When *they* had brought their *boats* to shore, *they* left everything and followed him' (my emphasis). The unnamed person is, of course, Andrew. Other characters, then, are involved, but Luke chooses to tell the story in such a way that all the attention is on Simon Peter.

4 The leper

Luke 5:12–16

The outline of this story is vague. As in Matthew (8:1–4) and Mark (1:40–45) the man is given no name. This is usual in the Gospels, but not inevitable: Mark 10:46–52 tells us of Bartimaeus, and even gives us his father's name, although Luke 18:35–43 leaves him anonymous, and so does Matthew, who has 'two blind men' (20:29–34). With Bartimaeus, too, we know the healing took place somewhere near Jericho (Luke 18:35 has 'As he approached Jericho…'; Matthew 20:29 says 'As they were leaving Jericho…'; and Mark 10:46 mentions Jesus' arrival and departure from Jericho). With this leper, we don't have any clear idea of where the encounter took place.

It is natural for us to speculate as to why this is so vague. Didn't Luke have any historical knowledge? Was there no name in the original story to avoid drawing attention to the man, who might otherwise have had his life endangered in the early days after Jesus' death? This hardly explains the lack of precision about place and time. In the end we have to admit we don't know the reasons for the vagueness. However, it does ensure the story is read emblematically, as an illustration of how Jesus fulfilled his claim in the synagogue in Nazareth. Although there was a specific leper, he is also representative of all other lepers that Jesus healed.

There are also some interesting specifics. First, Luke describes him as 'covered with leprosy'; the other Gospel writers don't. This may be an indication of Luke's medical awareness. It certainly emphasises the significance of the healing—there could be no doubt if all the leprosy disappeared. But all the Gospels note Jesus' instruction for him to go and be checked out by the priest, as instructed in the Law (see Leviticus 13 and 14 for all kinds of intricate details). The phrase 'for a testimony to *them*' (v. 14, my emphasis) is noteworthy. While the plural may refer to the priests, it reads as though this healing is a testimony to the priests and people about the healings of Jesus. Certainly that is the consequence as more and more people learn about Jesus, listen to him and are healed. Typically, too, Jesus withdraws for solitude and prayer.

5 The paralysed man

Luke 5:17–26

This is a very appealing and potent story containing important and well-known insights about the healing ministry of Jesus. Healing was dependent on God's power (v. 17); it was about spiritual issues such as forgiveness (v. 20); and it was enabled by friendship and faith (vv. 18–20). Also, Jesus displayed amazing insight both into the real need of the paralysed man (v. 20) and the poisoned minds of 'the scribes and the Pharisees' (v. 21). Jesus' healings are also critical for underscoring his claim to be 'the Son of Man' (v. 24) and his divine authority, which provoked such deep antagonism among these religious leaders. The result of this healing is that both the man and the crowd 'glorified God' (v. 26). That is, they gave God the true and proper acknowledgement he warrants, as the angels did outside Bethlehem and as the shepherds did when they saw the infant Christ (2:14, 20). All of these are significant topics to explore; we, however, will focus on a less obvious matter.

In different ways, all of the last four stories (including this one) make the same point. The popularity of Jesus as a healer is growing and this is putting significant pressure on him. He seeks to focus on the preaching and as necessary withdraws for prayer (see 4:42–44; 5:1, 15–17). This growing popularity is not presented as the main theme (there is no standard way of recounting it) but it tells its own story and explains why the religious leaders had gathered from far and wide (v. 17). Nevertheless, in the process a significant change of focus has happened. While Jesus was preaching in the synagogues in 4:15, 16 and 44, first in Galilee and then (according to some manuscripts) in Judea, in chapter 5 Jesus is exercising his ministry outside the synagogues. Although in his warnings about future persecutions he speaks of disciples being put out of the synagogues (that is, forbidden to enter them), it is unlikely that this was Jesus' own experience, for in 6:6 he is situated in a synagogue once again. Rather this is Luke's way of indicating that Jesus' ministry is now no longer confined either to the synagogues or to sabbaths. It is going on all the time.

6 Party time

This section forms the conclusion of a chiasm in chapter 5—or in less technical terms a sandwich-like structure. The outside sections (the 'bread') are two stories about Jesus calling disciples. The first is about 'the four', but especially Peter (5:1–11); the second is about the call of Levi. The 'filling' consists of two significant healing stories—the leper and the paralysed man—both of which are about cleansing. One involves a physical cleansing with strong spiritual implications (as a leper the man was not permitted to join others in worshipping God); the other involves a spiritual cleansing with strong physical implications (people saw the man's paralysis but Jesus forgave his sins).

The reason for pointing this out is not merely to give general information. Rather it suggests a line of understanding for the call of Levi and especially the concluding epigram: 'Those who are well have no need of a physician, but those who are sick; I have come to call not the righteous but sinners to repentance' (vv. 31–32).

The obvious and direct way to understand Jesus' words here is to apply them to Levi (and his party friends), as the saying follows Levi's call and the Pharisees' criticism of Jesus' unseemly behaviour in associating with 'unclean' people. On this reading, the first line is understood metaphorically as applying to Levi (he is physically well but spiritually sick—he is betraying his nation and his name by collecting taxes for the Romans, and in the process, through regular contact with these pagans, he is intentionally making himself unclean). The second line then relates directly to Levi. Jesus is calling this sinful man to repent and follow him.

Without denying this reading of the text (vv. 31–32 are actually the response of Jesus to the question about eating and drinking with outcasts and so polluting himself), understanding it as the conclusion to a chiasm brings out another depth. Peter too, on his own admission, was a 'sinful man' (see 5:8). The two healings show Jesus as the physician healing the sick. But in fact the two men who are called to be his disciples are also in need of healing and repentance.

Verse 32 can then be related back to 4:18–19, where Jesus used verses from Isaiah 61 to provide an outline of his mission. Here we see, even more clearly, who Jesus regarded as 'the poor' who needed the 'good news'.

Guidelines

Jesus' claim in Luke 4 to be the one fulfilling Isaiah 61 is clearly pivotal for his mission as presented by Luke. How do you think Luke intends us to understand those words of prophecy? How important is it to read on into the Gospel to discover his meaning?

What does this prophecy suggest about Jesus' understanding of his mission? Is it socio-economic? National, involving political and military deliverance? Personal, involving healing and restoration?

Do you think Luke is intentionally presenting Jesus in a non-political light because of the person for whom he is writing the Gospel? Or is this a valid reflection of the way Jesus understood and carried out his mission?

The conclusions we reach about Jesus' mission ought to affect the kind of Christian we are and the activities in which we are involved. Think about how your Christian life reflects your understanding of Jesus. Do you need to consider making some adjustments?

To what extent does your church relate its life and mission to the mission of Jesus? If you could help the church take on one new mission or evangelism project, what would it be? Pray for your leaders (locally and nationally) as they grapple with the challenges of living authentically for Christ in our times.

FURTHER READING

E. Earle Ellis, *The Gospel of Luke* (*New Century Bible Commentary*) (Eerdmans, 1974).

I. Howard Marshall, *The Gospel of Luke* (*New International Greek Testament Commentary*) (Paternoster, 1979).

John Nolland, *Luke 1—9:20* (*Word Bible Commentary*) (Word, 1989).

Tom Wright, *Luke for Everyone* (SPCK, 2001).

Hebrews

Why read or study the letter to the Hebrews? It has no obvious author, few of us are Hebrew and there's a lot of the Bible to be reading! What's more, it is not clear what it is for or what it is about. The Gospels tell us about Jesus' life; the letters of Paul and others are addressed to early-church communities and address their concerns and problems; Acts is self-explanatory; and Revelation is a liturgical unveiling of both the present and the end times. The letter to the Hebrews, by contrast, is rather obscure. It gives a lot of time over to talking about angels, the ritual of the temple and the Old Testament priesthood, none of which—at least at first sight—seem immediately relevant to our Christian discipleship.

Yet one of the great biblical scholars and bishops of the late 19th and early 20th centuries, Brooke Foss Westcott, wrote of the letter to the Hebrews, 'The more I study the tendencies of the time in some of the busiest centres of life, the more deeply I feel that the Spirit of God warns us of our most urgent civil and spiritual dangers through the Epistle to the Hebrews.'

If life was busy and there were civil and spiritual dangers in 1892 (when those words were written) then how much more relevant will this text be for us today? What's more, not only might we find through further study that angels, the temple and the priesthood are not half as far away from our present concerns as we first thought, but the letter closes by addressing the themes of faith and hope. There is no place and no time when these abiding virtues are not important, and we will spend the next fortnight well if at the close of it we have come to a better understanding of them.

Quotations are taken from the New Revised Standard Version of the Bible.

1 What's in a name?

Hebrews 13:22–25

Why do people's names seem so important to us? One of the first things we do when we meet someone is exchange names. Knowing someone's name is a sign of our care for and attentiveness to them. When Anglicans are confirmed the bishop says to them, 'God has called you by name and made you his own.' To know a name is in part to know a person and at least to have a connection with them.

The letter to the Hebrews is unique among New Testament texts in that we have no idea of the name of its author. Whatever scholars may debate about how many of Paul's letters were by him or who the John was who wrote the book of Revelation, we at least have a name at the top of the work. The letter to the Hebrews, however, stands mysteriously silent as to its authorship. Written for a Jewish audience (hence the name) it is only really a letter in its title. In all other respects we'd call it a short book or an address. It doesn't begin with a greeting, as so many of the other letters do, and it is only at the end, as the author says, 'I want you to know that our brother Timothy has been set free' (v. 23), that we are given any indication of human interest.

It's the reference to Timothy that has led a number of writers and scholars over the centuries to ascribe the text to Paul, given his close association with someone of the same name in several other New Testament letters. While it sounds unlike Paul's style, it still may be by him. It certainly doesn't contradict any of his great themes and is on the same level of sophistication and sweep as his letter to the Romans. More likely, however, is that it is by one of his pupils or associates. Theologians in the third century suggested Barnabas, and later on they wondered if it might be by Apollos, to whom Paul refers in his first letter to the Corinthians (1 Corinthians 3:6). Whoever the author is, however, we can say with confidence that he was inspired by the Holy Spirit, and whatever the writer's name, the name to which the whole work points is abundantly clear: Jesus.

2 Living in the last days

Hebrews 1:1–3

People in every age imagine that their age is the worst. Thomas Arnold in the 1830s thought nothing could save the Church of England, and at the height of the banking crisis in 2008 there were plenty of people predicting the end of the economic world as we knew it. At some point, of course, things will end, if only when the sun dies in five billion years or so. The Bible is full of what theologians call eschatology—beliefs about the end of the world—and the New Testament has plenty of warnings from Jesus about not presuming to know when the end will be.

The letter to the Hebrews, which scholars think was written either just before or just after the destruction of the temple in Jerusalem by the Romans, was speaking to people keenly aware of the tumult of the age and the dark significance of the razing of the centre of Jewish life. When the letter says 'but in these last days he has spoken to us by a Son' (v. 2) it is speaking partly about the end of the traditional way of life focused on the temple and the end of the world as it was known.

Yet this is about more than just an isolated historical event. The letter to the Hebrews teaches us that we live right now in 'these last days'. Ever since the death and resurrection of Jesus we have been living in the last days. If the first days were before God's covenant with his people Israel, and the middle days were the days of that covenant, then the days lived in the light of the resurrection are the last days. They are the last days precisely because God, who spoke in earlier days by the prophets, now speaks through a Son. There is no further covenant or revelation to be made, for what could supersede the incarnation, the coming among us of God himself?

Whenever we worry about what is round the corner or how things will end, we should recall that we already live in the last days and all is in Jesus' hands, whatever the prophets of doom may say. The worst that can happen, the crucifixion, has already happened.

3 Angels and abasement

Popular belief in hell and sin is not what it once was; few preachers attract converts to the Christian faith by conjuring up images of hellfire, or working up their audience into paroxysms of guilt like the splendidly named Father Furnace (an English Roman Catholic priest) used to in the 19th century! One of the elements of traditional Christianity that retains its popularity, however, is angels. The author of Hebrews lived in a world similarly open to the angelic, but remained clear that Jesus was no mere angel. Most of the first chapter of the letter is given over to demonstrating, with several quotations from the Psalms, that the predicted Messiah was a Son in and through whom all things were made. At the end of chapter 1 the writer puts it plainly: angels are sent to serve those of us being saved by the Son, not to be the saviour themselves.

Having exalted Jesus as utterly superior to the angels, the letter then takes a different direction and spends the entirety of chapter 2 indicating the humility of Jesus: exaltation through abasement. This is important work because the people who said at the crucifixion, 'He saved others; let him save himself' (Luke 23:35) were not alone. If this great and glorious Jesus really is the Son of God, then how does the ignominy of suffering and death fit into the scheme of things? Why did he not just overthrow and smite his enemies? Angels may have retained their popularity but humility has never been fashionable.

The nature of and reason for Jesus' abasement and death will be worked out in the succeeding chapters. Here the author of the letter makes one thing clear: we begin with the fact that Jesus identifies with us; it is fitting that Jesus should suffer because *we* suffer: 'For the one who sanctifies and those who are sanctified all have one Father' (2:11). Jesus came to human beings, not angels, and he is not ashamed to call us his brothers and sisters, we're told; he came to free us from slavery, and because he was tested he is able to help us when we are tested. He who is beyond the angels, who is the Son of God, has come and shared our lot. From the beginning of the letter the author wants us to know Jesus is on our side.

4 Keep on keeping on

Hebrews 3:1—4:13

However strong our faith, it can't help but be affected by events around us and in our lives. When we lose a loved one, while our faith should be a light and a comfort to us, we would be unusual (to say the least) if we did not ask questions and have moments of grief and doubt. There are times when so many hard events happen, one after another, that we can feel tempted to give up. All the normal comforts and anchors in our lives have gone or seem no longer secure, and we do not know which way to turn.

For the recipients of this letter the same was true. They had been undergoing persecution and were expecting to face it again. While we do not know if Hebrews was written before or after the destruction of the Jerusalem temple in AD70, it is clear that this was a profoundly unsettling time for the readers.

The author of Hebrews, therefore, returns constantly to a refrain about not falling away and being patient, writing, 'We have become partners of Christ, if only we hold our first confidence firm to the end' (3:14). The theme of unity with Jesus is continued but now as an encouragement not to lose heart or fall away. There is that thing a persecuted or under-pressure group of people long for more than anything else: rest. This will come, we are told, provided we keep faith and continue to strive amid our various trials. Just like the last days being now and continuing to be now, so the rest that was once offered to Joshua and his people is still not achieved and so is still available, unclaimed. 'If Joshua had given them rest,' we're told, 'God would not speak later about another day' (4:8). Rest still remains for the people of God, we are assured, not least because God has willed 'they would not, apart from us, be made perfect' (11:40). Joshua's failure might even have been providential. Just as rest remained open to the Hebrews it remains open to us who, by our baptism, are also partners of Christ. Amid our trials we should lift our heads up and behold that rest being held out to us, to Joshua and to the first recipients of this letter, all together in Jesus Christ.

5 The family business

Hebrews 4:14—5:10

When my Dad was at school he had an elderly careers teacher who had once worked for Pilkington Glass. He felt it his duty, therefore, not only to send his own sons to work for the firm but to encourage every boy who came for careers advice to work for Pilkington too. Whatever desires or aptitudes a boy came with, he was sure to find they were suited to working in the glass business!

We think today of the priesthood as being something to which people are called. Churches spend a lot of time and money encouraging and discerning vocations to ordained ministry. Yet in the time prior to Jesus Christ, the priesthood was nothing of the sort. Instead it was something to be inherited—a family business. The ministry of being a priest was given to Levi and then Aaron and his family, so it was only possible to be a priest by inheritance and descent. Jesus' relative Zechariah was a priest, but Jesus was of the house of Judah not Levi and so was not. Judah, of course, was the royal tribe, the house from which David was descended, and so it indicates something to us of Jesus' royal identity: he is the new King David.

Yet the writer of Hebrews unequivocally calls Jesus a 'great high priest' (v. 14). The facts on the ground, so to speak, meant the author could do nothing else. Jesus had offered his life to the Father and so, pre-eminently, was a priest—sacrificing not something else but his very self. The question, however, was how? What we are being introduced to here is not only a different and mysterious priest, but the beginnings of a new way of thinking about worship. Until the coming of Christ, worship was something done by a particular caste on behalf of everyone else; in the light of Jesus' death and resurrection, worship is something all are called to. The ordained ministry is still a family business, but the family is the church. We don't inherit this ministry, but some are called to preside at the worship of God's people.

6 Melchize-who?

Hebrews 7:1–22

There are certain names from the Bible we know well: Adam, Eve, Moses, David, Mary and so on. One name that's less likely to come immediately to our consciousness is Melchizedek. Yet this name is at the centre of the letter to the Hebrews. The author of the letter is aware that even its Hebrew readers may need a little reminding, so quotes almost in full the text from the book of Genesis (14:18–20) where we learn that Abraham encounters a king who is also a priest, who blesses him and to whom Abraham gives one-tenth of his possessions. That priest-king is called Melchizedek. The same priest-king occurs one more time in the Old Testament, in Psalm 110:4, when God tells David's lord (whoever he is) that he is 'a priest forever according to the order of Melchizedek'.

Other than these two references we know nothing about this person. The letter to the Hebrews is very clear that he is immensely significant, for even the patriarch Abraham gives him tithes, and Abraham, through whom all the nations are to be blessed, himself receives a blessing from this priest-king. We know he was king of Salem, which means 'peace', and that King Melchizedek means 'king of righteousness'; so we have a priest-king of enormous significance who is king of peace and righteousness, whom David refers to as his lord but who is not the Lord God of the Old Testament and Psalms. In other words, the author of the letter tells us, we have Jesus (see Hebrews 5:6).

Suddenly it becomes clear how Jesus can be a priest despite being descended from David: he is a priest forever according to the order of Melchizedek, not Levi. We hear little of this priesthood but, when we do hear of it (in Genesis and the Psalms), it is of tremendous importance. The author of Hebrews wants us to know that this is the priesthood held by Jesus, and it is from this fact that so much of the rest of this letter proceeds. Despite his dimly remembered name, the one whom even the patriarch Abraham revered is rather more important than indicated by the number of references he has in the Bible. It is perhaps a gentle reminder to us that in God's economy the truly significant are not always those about whom most is said or who have the most to say for themselves.

Guidelines

In this first week we've learned something of the mysteriousness of the letter to the Hebrews: its authorship and the identity of the priest Melchizedek. We have discovered something too of the importance of perseverance amid trials. Above all, we have hopefully begun to see how this letter is for us: how we also are living in the last days and how Jesus abases himself for us and comes alongside us in our suffering.

As Hebrews prompts us to ponder the angels, we might ask what role they play in our lives. Do we call on the assistance of our guardian angel (Matthew 18:10), and are we conscious when we are at worship—especially at the eucharist—that we are in the presence of angels? Amid the many reasons for angels is the fact that they are a constant reminder of an invisible world beyond this visible one, also created by God, of which the Nicene Creed speaks. It was the angels who sang 'Glory to God in the highest' (Luke 2:14) on Christmas night, so perhaps we should ask them to assist us in giving glory to God in the daily routine of our lives.

1 The final priest

Hebrews 7:23–28

There was no shortage of priests in Old Testament times, and they had a lot of work to do. There were the daily offerings and burnings of incense, and then the annual offering at Yom Kippur (the Day of Atonement) involving bulls, goats and rams. The priests, being sinners, needed to offer sacrifices for their own sins before they could offer them for those of other people. What was more, the sacrifices needed repeating, because they couldn't achieve atonement once and for all. Finally, the priests were human beings and so died, of course, and needed replacing.

Priests who were themselves sinners; insufficient offerings; priests who died out: these problems with the worship of God needed to be solved by a different kind of priest. Jesus Christ, says the letter to the Hebrews, is that priest.

Jesus' priesthood is of a different order. He is without sin ('holy, blameless, undefiled' (v. 26)) and so does not need to offer sacrifices for his own sins first. He is also resurrected from the dead ('he continues forever' (v. 24)) and so is not prevented from exercising his priesthood by death. Finally, he did not offer animal flesh and blood to God but human flesh and blood: 'he offered himself' (v. 27). God takes human flesh in order to offer it back to himself, in order to present an offering that is at last whole, complete and worthy.

This priesthood follows that of Melchizedek. As we have seen, Psalm 110 (the most-quoted Old Testament text in the New Testament) speaks of God telling some future lord of David to sit at his right hand, and says that God has sworn an unchangeable oath that this lord is a priest forever according to the order of Melchizedek. The author of our letter (together with the early church as a whole) saw this psalm as prophetic, alluding to Jesus Christ as the one who would ascend to sit at God's right hand after making the perfect offering to God on earth. All that the Old Testament priesthood alluded to or prefigured is now fulfilled and completed in the final priest, Jesus Christ our Lord.

2 Sacred space

Hebrews 9:1–5

Ask several people to describe a traditional church building and you would probably get broadly similar answers. People would talk of a nave and a chancel and probably of a sanctuary; a font and an altar would feature and very possibly an organ and bells. Ask one of Jesus' countrymen to describe the temple and they would have given you an even clearer answer: an outer court, an inner court and finally, separated by a blue curtain, a Holy of Holies. Chapter 9 of the letter to the Hebrews explains the make-up of the temple in some detail, for this was not only the centre of religion for Jesus' compatriots but it was known very well to God's people, given most of them made an annual pilgrimage there. The writer describes not the temple of masonry, whose western wall we can still see in Jerusalem today, but the tent (v. 2) that formed the original tabernacle, the forerunner of the temple outlined in the book of Exodus (Exodus 35—40 is given over almost entirely to a detailed description of the tabernacle and its construction).

By Jesus' time the Holy of Holies in the stone temple in Jerusalem probably no longer contained Aaron's rod or the manna, but it still contained the cherubim surrounding the ark or box in which they had stood, and which may have still contained the tablets of the ten commandments.

The temple was a microcosm of creation. The inner court represented earth, and the Holy of Holies represented heaven, while the blue curtain separating them represented the sky—the veil between heaven and earth. Anything done in the temple was therefore done to the whole of creation: in blessing and sprinkling the temple with life-giving blood, the priests were blessing and renewing the world that the temple represented. How often when we are in church do we think of ourselves as engaging in the work of renewing all creation? Jesus' body is the new temple and we are his body: our offerings of prayer and praise, and supremely our celebration of the eucharist, are doing the same renewing work—only more excellently. That should keep us awake next time our eyelids droop on a Sunday morning.

3 Blood brothers

Hebrews 9:8–22

We could be forgiven for thinking our letter-writer has an obsession with blood, going on and on about sprinkled blood and offerings of blood before finally, in verse 22, coming out with what this has all been pointing to: 'without the shedding of blood there is no forgiveness of sins'. Blood was always being spilt in the many temple sacrifices and never more importantly so than on the Day of Atonement, when the high priest made his annual entry to the Holy of Holies beyond the curtain to sprinkle blood on the curtain and the mercy seat holding the ark of the covenant.

We could imagine this to be rather childish: demanding blood for forgiveness sounds barbaric and unchristian, something the world should grow out of, like bear-baiting or cock-fighting. Yet the shedding of blood is all around us, not least in so-called honour-killings and revenge murders. The shedding of blood as a response to sin or perceived sin is far from being a relic of the past; it's as present as ever. In the period of the temple it was far from ineffective: Hebrews informs us that the sprinkling of goats' and bulls' blood and cows' ashes 'sanctifies those who have been defiled so that their flesh is purified' (v. 13). What's more, in the temple it was not the blood of humans being shed but the blood of animals. God's command is that those made in his image should *not* be killed (one of the ten commandments lodged in the temple explicitly prohibits murder), but rather that offerings should be made with animals. Indeed, God prevented Abraham from sacrificing his son and provided a ram instead (Genesis 22:12–13), and at the first Passover lambs' blood was to be smeared on the lintels of houses in place of the blood of the first-born Israelites (Exodus 12:13).

But why blood? Blood represented life. It was the ultimate offering to God, signifying the giving-up of the most precious thing—the life that he himself had given. It was a sign of love and commitment. Through animal blood, however, 'the way into the sanctuary has not yet been disclosed' (v. 8), for Christ was to be the 'high priest of the good things that have come' (v. 11). Ultimately divine love and commitment meant that God, in Jesus, shed his own blood for us.

4 A sacrifice for all time

Hebrews 10:1–18

It's funny how little details sometimes strike us. Curtains or blinds still closed at lunchtime can make us wonder if someone is ill, for example. At the crucifixion of Jesus we have what looks like a minor detail—'the curtain of the temple was torn in two' (Luke 23:45)—amid all the extraordinary drama of that afternoon. Yet this little observation is central to the death of Jesus. The curtain, you'll recall, separated the inner court from the Holy of Holies in the temple and represented the barrier between heaven and earth. It was the death of Jesus, his offering of his body and blood to the Father in love, that meant God forgave our sins and so reunited heaven and earth.

As we've seen before, that could only happen once. Jesus offered himself rather than something else; he is resurrected so cannot die; and he is sinless. In Jesus' offering at Jerusalem in the midst of the real creation rather than the temple, all the offerings of old—'a shadow of the good things to come and not the true form of these realities' (v. 1)—are fulfilled and completed. 'By a single offering he has perfected for all time those who are sanctified,' we are told (v. 14): sin is finally defeated and Jesus need never be crucified again.

Yet we all know that we still suffer from the consequences of sin and we still sin ourselves. The victory of the cross has not yet worked itself out through history, and the triumph of 2000 years ago needs to be made present for us now in the midst of our troubles. That's why Jesus instituted the eucharist on the night before his sacrificial death: so that his once-for-all victory may be made present for the generations to come. For, as the author of Hebrews puts it in the final chapter, while looking forward to the future, 'We have an altar' too (13:10). In the sacraments of the new temple—the body of Jesus into which we've been baptised (10:22)—Jesus' sacrifice made once for all time is made present for us now. Ours is no mere faith in a past event, but a present share in 'an indestructible life' (7:16).

5 Faith that moves mountains

Hebrews 11

Our faith is what the eucharist sustains and what carries us towards the heavenly city (vv. 14–16), to which God has called us in Jesus Christ. Chapter 11 of the letter to the Hebrews is not only a masterly summary of the forward movement of the Old Testament, but a poetic and moving account of how the saints of every generation have achieved, by God's grace, the most astonishing things. Yet at the same time these saints will not finally be saved and made perfect without us (v. 40). We discover that the blood of Jesus makes us brothers and sisters not just of him and one another but of all those in the centuries before who have lived by faith.

The gift of faith, we are told, is 'the assurance of things hoped for, the conviction of things not seen' (v. 1)—those things being the heavenly city and the rest that we are promised. This assurance or conviction achieves amazing results, as the panegyric in verses 32–38 makes clear. These are people of whom the world is not worthy indeed. It is a wonderful reminder to us that goodness is so much more joyful and exciting and life-giving than evil. Theologians have often observed that tyrants are not only all the same but are all ultimately rather banal (a word we might especially associate with Hannah Arendt, whose 1963 book *Eichmann in Jerusalem: A report on the banality of evil* powerfully demonstrated this observation). One imagines going for a walk with Hitler or Stalin and then rapidly finding tedious their obsession with the great leap forward, or *lebensraum*, or the manifest superiority of the Soviet system, or whatever. The saints, however, summarised in their actions by verses 32–38, are anything but monomaniacal. The sheer range of their lives, work and endurance is breathtaking and thrilling. I have those seven verses printed out and framed on my desk as a reminder when I become crabby or cynical about what we Christians are capable of. I recommend it! As this beautiful prayer says:

Almighty and everlasting God, who hast enkindled the flame of love in the hearts of thy saints: grant to us the same faith and power of love that we, rejoicing in their triumphs, may be sustained by their example and fellowship; through Jesus Christ our Lord. Amen.

Collect for Fourth Sunday before Advent, *Common Worship*

6 You'll never walk alone

Hebrews 12

Just as the eucharist makes present for us the once-for-all sacrificial death of Jesus, so our baptism makes present in our lives those who have gone before us in Christ. Verse 1 gives us the image of running in a race, surrounded in the stadium by all those people of whom the letter-writer has already spoken—the heroes of the past—who cheer and encourage us on.

The author is well aware that the first readers, like ourselves, are prone to 'grow weary or lose heart' (v. 3) and encourages us not just with the prayers of the saints but also with the supreme example of our Lord himself. This is done not just by appealing to duty and endurance, but by reminding us of the prize—the same 'joy that was set before [Jesus]' (v. 2) and drew him on. So often we can't imagine God laughing or being joyful, and yet we see here the joy of God that spurred Christ on to finish his work—the final joy of returning to the bosom of the Father (John 1:18). The same destination awaits us.

We are reminded too that the glory and splendour of the old covenant is not lost but rather is even more glorious and splendid. The cult of the temple was nothing if not spectacular ('a blazing fire, and darkness, and gloom, and a tempest, and the sound of a trumpet' (v. 18)). However at the Christian altar, and by sharing in the body of him who is already seated at the right hand of the Father, we have come to something yet more extraordinary: 'the city of the living God... and to innumerable angels in festal gathering, and to the assembly of the firstborn who are enrolled in heaven... and to Jesus, the mediator of a new covenant' (vv. 22–24).

Precisely because in our worship we no longer come to earthly shadows and anticipations of the future, but to share 'with angels and archangels and all the company of heaven' (as the prefaces to Anglican eucharistic prayers put it) in the true kingdom of the world to come, this is something solid and permanent. It is not something that can be 'shaken' (v. 28); it is something we can trust and to which we can give our hearts and lives. It is exactly the 'sure and steadfast anchor' (6:19) spoken of before.

Guidelines

We have not only had set out for us the mystery of the atonement and Jesus' fulfilment and completion of the worship and sacrifices of old, but we have learned that this eternal atonement is made present for us now in our worship and, although we have not come to something that can be seen, nonetheless our worship truly is an anticipation of heaven. Precisely because of that, our faith, nurtured by the eucharist and encouraged by our brothers and sisters gone before us, is a great golden thread drawing us towards the joy of the kingdom, the unutterable bliss of union with God.

So many of the images and themes of this week are echoed and given vivid illustration in our Christian sacramental worship, where we share with Jesus in the labour of blessing, renewing and restoring an ailing and sinful creation. How often are we aware that this is what we are doing each time we celebrate Holy Communion? Are we conscious that when we reconcile others or forgive someone who has done us wrong we are engaged in a cosmically significant act, like the sprinkling of blood in the temple—except even better? This conviction should give us renewed zeal for the protection of the environment and our local communities, together with working and praying for peace, as those who share in the royal priesthood of Jesus Christ.

FURTHER READING

Margaret Barker, *Temple Theology: An introduction* (SPCK, 2004).

Matthew Levering, *Sacrifice and Community: Jewish offering and Christian eucharist* (Blackwell, 2005).

Jane Williams, *Angels* (Lion Hudson, 2006).

Tom Wright, *Hebrews for Everyone* (SCM Press, 2003).

Jonah

Jonah is quite a comical story. God tells a prophet to get up and go to Nineveh; so he gets up and goes—in the opposite direction! The prophet of the God of Israel meets foreign sailors who prove to be far more noble, prayerful and spiritually open than he is. Both the sailors and the people of Nineveh respond to Jonah's words with repentance—to which his own reaction is an angry sulk! There is an epic scale to the storm, the fish, the city and even Jonah's mood swings (the Hebrew word for 'great' keeps recurring). All this gives a somewhat cartoonish feel to the tale, as does the total repentance of Nineveh, from the people and king down to the lowliest animals. There is much here that seems intended to raise a smile.

But humour can have a sharp edge. Those who claim to be God's people, and particularly those who are called to speak God's message, will find serious challenges in Jonah. The book asks questions about our obedience, our prejudices, our temptation to feel superior or resentful, and our whole understanding of how God relates to us and the rest of creation. Along with the humour, there is a disturbing, tragic element to Jonah's attitudes and actions.

Is the book of Jonah more than simply a funny story? Some insist that the events described in it should all be taken literally, and provide examples of mariners who have survived long periods inside sea creatures. Others point out that the story is deliberately vague about historical details and 'larger than life' in content, with brilliant use of structure, irony and rhetoric, so they read it as a parable or a 'didactic story'. Ultimately, the question of historicity is irrelevant to the interpretation of the book. The writer's real concern is that readers should hear the message, not for them to argue about whether the events actually happened!

The author of the book is not identified. As to its date, it refers to Nineveh, the capital of Assyria, which began threatening Israel in the mid-eighth century BC. Some scholars argue that it was written after the Babylonian exile, since phrases such as 'God of heaven' (1:9) are most common in post-exilic literature.

Quotations are taken from the New Revised Standard Version.

21–27 March

1 Escaping the call

Jonah 1:1–3

Most prophetic books centre on the message of the prophet. This one gives us almost nothing of the message, focusing instead on actions. It tells the story of a very reluctant prophet.

Jonah is described simply as the 'son of Amittai' (v. 1); with these minimal family details, we launch straight into his adult life. A 'Jonah son of Amittai' is also mentioned in 2 Kings 14:25, identified as a northern prophet who correctly predicted that Israel would recapture territory from Syria. That Jonah prophesied shortly before Assyria became a major threat to Israel.

YHWH, God of Israel ('LORD' in most English Bibles), tells Jonah to get up and go east, to Nineveh. Jonah does the opposite, taking a boat to the far west of the known world. What is Jonah thinking and feeling as he makes this choice? Putting ourselves in his shoes, we may initially guess that he is simply afraid of venturing into a vast and hostile city to 'cry out against it' (v. 2) and so confront its wrongdoing, and we may well sympathise—it seems a tall order, and a truly daunting prospect. But there is more to Jonah's reluctance than simply fear, as we shall see later.

Jonah tries to 'flee… from the presence of YHWH' (mentioned twice in verse 3 and also in verse 10). Perhaps he hopes that putting himself out of the picture will prompt God to choose some other prophet to preach to Nineveh, leaving him to get on with his life in peace. Or maybe Jonah shares the view, common in ancient times, that deities are most powerful in their own locations, where they are known and worshipped—so distance from YHWH's land means at least some degree of freedom from YHWH's control. If that is Jonah's idea, he needs to discover a much bigger picture of God (compare Psalm 139:7–12).

Resisting God's call is a recurring theme in the Old Testament (think of Moses, Gideon, Saul, Jeremiah, Israel as the 'servant' in Isaiah). It can be tempting for us too—perhaps by turning our backs on God, or else trying to drown out God's voice by immersing ourselves in busyness.

2 Going down!

Jonah 1:4–17

Certain words are repeated for effect in this book; one of them is 'down'. Jonah goes down to Joppa; down into the ship; down into the hold. As the wind and the waves rise up, the sailors are aware of the imminent danger, while Jonah sinks deeper into a stupefying sleep. Finally Jonah is thrown down into the sea, and slides down the throat of the fish. Here is a man on a downward path—an image which might prompt in us thoughts of decline, or depression, or death and burial.

A crisis can be transformational. In the storm, the cargo—the sailors' precious livelihood—is thrown overboard. When your ship is about to sink, your values and priorities are suddenly changed and clarified. The sailors turn to prayer, as best they can; the captain has to wake up Jonah and urge him to pray (echoing YHWH's word to Jonah at the start of the book, 'Arise!').

Quizzing their puzzling passenger, the sailors discover that the god from whom he is running is not simply a territorial god resident in Israel, but a universal sovereign ruling over land and sea. They see the implications: who can hope to run from such a god? The sailors give up calling on their various gods and turn to YHWH, combining respect for human life with honest and fervent prayer. Another of the story's amusing ironies emerges: through Jonah's words, and despite his unwillingness, these pagan sailors come to faith in YHWH! The truths which this reluctant missionary speaks have an impact, in spite of the speaker's very obvious failings. The sovereign God sometimes works in ways that can raise a wry smile.

This passage shares a number of similarities with Psalm 107:23–32. There the outcome of being saved from a stormy sea is to give thanks and praise to YHWH. The sailors in our story have responded that way, like model Israelites; now how will this Israelite prophet Jonah respond? And what about us, the readers—how will we choose to respond? What might God want to teach us through those who do not share our faith, not least during times of crisis?

3 Singing in the depths

Jonah 2

The confused, idol-worshipping foreigners have shown the way, in integrity, honesty and prayer. Now, at last, we find the one who knows the living God turning to prayer!

Jonah's poetic prayer would fit well in the book of Psalms, with its account of God's rescuing him from deep trouble, as well as its mention of the temple (vv. 4, 7). We cannot tell whether this is a song Jonah makes up himself, or one he has learned previously. Perhaps it was a favourite of the writer of the book, for personal reasons. Believers down the centuries have found that crises can prompt powerful song-writing, while treasured songs or psalms which have been memorised can themselves nourish and sustain us during a crisis.

Jonah senses YHWH's hand in these traumatic events. He knows that the sailors reluctantly threw him overboard, yet says it is YHWH who 'cast me into the deep' (v. 3). As he was sinking into Sheol, the mysterious place of the dead, it was YHWH's waves that swept over him, and YHWH who answered his cry for help. Through it all, YHWH is sovereign, and listens to those who call.

The content of Jonah's psalm is striking. Overall, it sounds good, orthodox in theology and wonderfully positive. He recounts his own experience of ordeal and rescue, ending with a promise of thanksgiving and worship in future. But there is no element of confession; Jonah happily recognises and receives God's grace, but does not seem to recognise his own sin, which has led him to his current predicament. He seems to assume that his relationship with God is healthy.

The idol-worshippers whom Jonah dismisses here (vv. 8–9) have thus far proved more righteous than him, doing the very things he now promises to do (1:14–16). Is Jonah really returning to 'true loyalty' (v. 8), or is his perspective still warped? Could he himself, ironically, be worshipping his own idols of national pride or of delight in God's judgement on his enemies? Will worshipping this gracious God who loves to save lead Jonah to become more like the one he worships, changing his own character? The proof will come, not in Jonah's words, but in his actions…

4 The God of second chances

Jonah 3:1–10

Chapter 3 opens with words almost identical to those with which the book began—except that now the word of YHWH comes to Jonah 'a second time'. Here is the God who gives second chances: Jonah has an opportunity to recommit to his calling, and through him the people of Nineveh will also have an opportunity to make a fresh start.

YHWH's vision and care extend to all he has created; divine blessing is for all nations (Genesis 12:3; Isaiah 45:22–23). The mission of such a God extends far beyond the boundaries of Israel (see Isaiah 19:24–25). The real missionary in this book is YHWH, whose determination to save overrules human failings. Yet still YHWH chooses to use human beings, with all their frailty, to get the job done.

We are given only one brief phrase from Jonah's preaching (v. 4). Is that all he said, both in proclamation and in any subsequent conversation? Presumably not; but it seems to be the central thrust of his message. Whether out of personal conviction or even a desire to sabotage the message, Jonah emphasises justice and judgement, rather than repentance and forgiveness by YHWH, the gracious God of Israel. It is clear from YHWH's opening words to Jonah (1:2) that sin matters and must be dealt with—Nineveh's sin, and also that of Jonah and the people he represents. God can and will deal with sin—either in judgement or in a gracious response to repentance. Jonah seems passionately concerned for God's justice; it is the good news of God's grace that sticks in his throat.

The involvement of animals in the repentance is striking and intriguing (vv. 7–8). Humans and animals are interdependent, and their fates are somehow intertwined; both matter to God (note YHWH's final words in 4:11). He directs a fish, a plant, a worm and a wind, as well as working in the hearts of human beings. YHWH, the God of Israel, is also the God of the entire creation.

Now almost everyone has changed their minds and actions: the sailors, the Ninevites, the king—even God, who decides not to destroy Nineveh after all, because of its response (compare Jeremiah 18:5–10). Only Jonah remains. In the light of events, will he also be open to change?

5 Scandalised by God's grace

Jonah 4:1–11

Jonah is totally enraged. Why? Is it because YHWH has made him a laughing stock, or even a false prophet, by not enforcing the promise of judgement? Or is it Jonah's nationalistic prejudice against 'ungodly' foreigners? Race may well be a factor: in his first words in the book, Jonah identifies himself ethnically as 'a Hebrew' (1:9). But there is more to it.

Now, as earlier, Jonah would rather die than repent of his convictions and attitudes (compare 1:12). In verse 2 he quotes one of the supreme revelations of YHWH's gracious character (Exodus 34:6), not with respect or even grudging admiration, but with frank disapproval. Jonah fails to realise that a prophet's success may ironically be seen in the non-fulfilment of what he threatened, as the hearers change their ways and God relents.

Twice YHWH asks Jonah what right he has to be angry—first, about the sparing of Nineveh, and then about the loss of the leafy bush which had shaded Jonah's hut from the blazing sun. Here is an object lesson for the prophet. Jonah cared about his own comfort, but not about the needs of others. If he cared about a plant, not wanting to see it die, should not God care about a whole city of people, not wanting to see them die? Is divine compassion only for us, not also for our enemies?

Jonah is happy to experience grace, but not to share it with others. His eloquent prayer of thanksgiving for his own rescue (ch. 2) is in stark contrast to his hypocritical resentment at the rescue of the people of Nineveh (ch. 4). 'Jonah wants to receive God's grace without being changed by it, and at the same time to snatch it away from those whose lives *are* in fact changed by it' (D.C. Timmer, *A Gracious and Compassionate God*, p. 133). The recurring personal pronouns I, me and my (nine times in this closing chapter) speak of self-righteousness.

How does the story end? The last word is an unanswered question. Indeed, there are 14 questions in these four short chapters, all of them directed at Jonah—and at the reader/listener, who identifies with him. Sharp questions can prompt us to deeper thought. Does Jonah repent, or not? We can never know; but we readers can answer the book's final question for ourselves. What will our response be to God's grace, and the light it sheds on our thinking and attitudes?

6 The sign of Jonah

Matthew 12:38–42

Jesus knew his scriptures, and found rich resources in them. In controversy with some of the religious leaders of his day, he looked to the Old Testament account of the Queen of Sheba (v. 42; 1 Kings 10), and also to the story of Jonah.

In the image of Jonah, lying in the great fish for three days and nights before emerging alive, Jesus finds a striking metaphor for his own forthcoming death and resurrection. In the repentance of the Ninevites, Jesus finds a challenge to people of his own day: if a notoriously reluctant and unreliable prophet could be used by God to provoke such a response in ancient times, how much more should Jesus' listeners repent as they see his actions and hear his preaching.

The account of Jonah might also resonate with Jesus' audience in other ways. Some of the scribes and Pharisees who confronted Jesus were clearly angered by his teaching and lifestyle, as he showed God's love to one and all—rather like Jonah, resisting the idea that God would be merciful to sinners, particularly Gentiles.

In this and other related passages referring to Jonah (Matthew 16:1–4; Luke 11:29–32), Jesus resists those who call for more 'signs', since they have already seen his miracles and heard his teaching. For those who have not responded, it seems that no sign will ever be powerful enough or convincing enough—although one more sign will still be given, the ultimate sign, his own death and resurrection. But for all who hear his words, the future remains open, and their responses will determine what follows. Jonah proclaimed judgement, yet the outcome was mercy. Jesus shows and proclaims mercy, but for those who reject such grace, the outcome will be judgement.

We may be inclined to sigh at many people's lack of biblical knowledge today. Yet we ourselves may neglect large portions of scripture. How often do we study or preach on the riches of the Old Testament? Exploring the Hebrew Bible can help us understand more deeply God's gracious nature and revelation, including the ultimate revelation in Christ.

Guidelines

As we enjoy the bittersweet humour of the book of Jonah, we may need to look in this mirror and laugh at ourselves—at the ways we misunderstand and misrepresent God; at our prejudices, blind spots and insidious self-righteousness; at our stubborn disobedience, and the way God can speak to us through seemingly unlikely people. What does Jonah show each of us that we particularly need to beware of, and to repent of?

With our perspective refreshed and restored by our interaction with Jonah's story, we can hear again God's invitation and challenge to be part of his mission. We can receive God's grace afresh, take delight in it, celebrate it—and look for opportunities to share it with others, through words and attitudes and actions.

The story itself can become a vehicle for mission, since Jonah has always been one of the best-known biblical characters. Early Christian catacombs and sarcophagi depict Jonah, as does the Sistine Chapel in Rome. Paintings, poems and oratorios down the years have explored his story. Sailors today still refer to someone whose presence may endanger the ship as 'a Jonah'. In Islam Jonah is known as Yunus, 'the one of the fish', and the Qur'an honours him as a prophet and a model of repentance. This widespread awareness of Jonah can give us points of contact with those who are not Christians. We might begin the conversation by asking if they know the story of Jonah. From there we could explore our common understanding of the story, and also what we see as most significant in the biblical account.

FURTHER READING:

G. Haslam, *The Jonah Complex* (Destiny Image, 2014).

R. Nixon, *The Message of Jonah* (IVP, 2003).

R.B. Salters, *Jonah and Lamentations* (Sheffield, 1994).

D.C. Timmer, *A Gracious and Compassionate God* (IVP, 2011).

To compare the accounts of Jonah in the Bible and the Qur'an,
   see www.bibleandkoran.net/verhaal.php?lIntEntityId=22

James

Contemporary Christians in the West seem to be finding the Bible increasingly hot to handle. Even Jesus' words cause concern where, for example, he speaks of divorce (Mark 10:1–12) and divine judgement (Mark 9:42–48). The Jesus tradition may lie at the heart of our faith but it has a habit of troubling us as his disciples. Many of us prefer a gospel of love without ethical ties—or at least the ones Jesus is recorded as having left us. We preach and believe in a loving and compassionate Jesus but find some of his teachings do not fit our understanding of love and compassion (for example, Matthew 7:21–23; 11:20–24). So we gloss over the difficult bits of Jesus' teaching, or we get worked up when they are raised. Others have found themselves disappointed at the words of Jesus because they tried them and found them not to work. None of this is new. James appears to have been grappling with the same issues in his letter.

The exact nature and purpose of the letter of James is disputed by scholars, and the debate is by no means over. However, most agree that James knows many sayings of Jesus and alludes to them in his letter. He grapples with the words of Jesus, trying to make sense of them within the experience of faith (and doubt and disappointment) of his audience and so discovering together with them their truth. These studies aim to open up the way James struggled with the words of Jesus and real life faith so that we can reflect on how we do the same today.

Quotations are taken from the NRSV where I have not used my own translations from the Greek.

1 Consider it nothing but joy

James 1:2–16

As an opening statement in a letter, James 1:2–4 is quite stark. While we do not know for sure whom James is addressing in his letter, we may make some reasonable assumptions about their lives from the text itself.

Some of them have little social status (v. 9), are desperately poor (2:15) and are humiliated in the church community (2:2–3). Some are suffering being at the wrong end of a nasty argument (4:1, 11) or grumbling gossip (5:9). James commands (not asks—note the Greek is an imperative) his fellow believers to consider their sufferings nothing but joy.

We do not know their reaction but we might be forgiven for speculating that this command might not go down too well—and James himself must have suspected this, given the infighting going on among them (4:1, 11; 5:9). He may well have expected some of that unpleasantness to come in his direction. However, this does not put him off making this command his opening remark. (His style is very different from that of Paul, who generally offers thanks for the many good things a congregation is involved in before addressing the difficult issues.)

Some English translations soften the blow by changing the word order and beginning the sentence with 'my brothers and sisters' or the acknowledgement of their suffering. James (as presented in the NIV) comes straight out with the command 'Consider it all joy' when you suffer. He takes his cue from Jesus, who commands his disciples to 'rejoice and be glad' in the very situations those James addresses are experiencing (Matthew 5:11–12). James captures the force of Jesus' saying with his 'all joy' (Greek: *pasan charan*), 'pure joy' or 'nothing but joy'. Given the normal human reaction to suffering, James's command seems tough.

However, James knows that something important—Christlike character— is at stake (vv. 3–4). He does not give the same reason for rejoicing in suffering as Jesus does (Matthew 5:12). To respond to suffering with bitterness and anger is to give in to evil (see 1:20). Rather, working through suffering with the faith that God too will be faithful produces the kind of tenacity that produces the kind of person who lives through all things with humble trust and grace—real Christian character.

2 Ask and it will be given to you

James 1:5–8, 17–25; 4:1–5

Members of the community are complaining that Jesus' words do not work. James's teaching on asking and not receiving (4:3) reflects Jesus' words that those who ask will receive (Matthew 7:7–11). Some in the community have tried this out, have asked but have not received. James picks up their disappointment.

James defends the words of Jesus against their accusations. His defence is twofold. First he states that some have not received because they do not ask (4:2). James expects his fellow Christians not simply to hear Jesus' words but to act on them (1:22–25). They cannot be angry with God for not answering prayers they have not prayed. Secondly he addresses those who have asked and not received. He states rather flatly that they have asked wrongly (4:3). His specific criticism is that they want to spend freely on their pleasures. The Greek term he uses (*dapanao*) has connotations of spending lavishly or extravagantly. James criticises the pseudo-spirituality of people who ask not for their needs or for those of others but for their own pleasures—and in abundance. (Paul makes the same criticism of some early Christians in 1 Timothy 6:5.)

In response to their criticisms of Jesus' words, James asks his fellow Christians to examine their own spirituality carefully. Are they acting out their faith in praying for their needs or simply complaining that they do not have what they want? Do they possess a Christlike spirituality of giving? Or is their character defined by selfish desire and greedy expectation? If so, they have become friends of the world and enemies of God.

James expects his fellow Christians to ask for God's wisdom and to do so with the full expectation that God will grant it and teach them how to live (1:5–8). Here again James interprets Jesus' saying (Matthew 7:7). Just as Jesus promised that the Father would give good gifts to those who ask (Matthew 7:11), so James affirms that the Father of lights is the source of all good gifts (1:17). He will give his wisdom to all who seek it unswervingly and then they will know better how to ask for good things.

3 You shall love your neighbour as yourself

James 2:1–13

The gospel of love is easily misunderstood. As we saw in yesterday's study, from the earliest times Christians have mistaken the love and generosity of God for a means to advance themselves financially and socially (1 Timothy 6:5), and this seems to have happened in the community James addresses. Some are so keen for self-advancement that they mistreat the poor and show the rich favour.

At one level this behaviour makes sense. These people believed themselves to be oppressed. They appear to have been dragged into court (v. 6). They suffer discrimination for their faith. The good name invoked over them is that of Christ and blasphemy against it implies some kind of discrimination against his followers (v. 7). Then as now, moving from a position of relative poverty and powerlessness was easier with friends in higher places, so it would serve their interests to make such friends.

James punctures this self-interest with the gospel of love. He draws on that command from Leviticus 19:18 which Jesus elevated to the second-greatest commandment—'you shall love your neighbour as yourself' (for example, Matthew 22:34–40). James points out that this law does not allow for partiality (v. 9). Whether it suits our interests or not, we should not show favouritism towards the rich. We must be at least as concerned about the poverty of others as we are about our own relative poverty.

He goes on to expound the nature of that gospel by recalling the words of Jesus in the beatitudes (Matthew 5:3–5). God has chosen the poor to inherit his kingdom (v. 5). Therefore treating the poor without respect is out of sync with the divine plan for salvation. Later in the epistle James suggests it makes us enemies of God (4:4). More to the point, it grants respect and honour to the chief perpetrators of injustice (2:6–7). Acting like this turns justice on its head. The gospel calls us to love all equally, even if that costs us personally in terms of our plans for self-improvement.

4 Justified by works and not by faith alone

James 2:14–26

Here James grapples not with the words of Jesus so much as with a particular interpretation of the words of Paul or somebody preaching something similar. Jesus praised people who had faith in him and he yearned to see faith in Israel (Matthew 8:10). Paul spoke of justification being through faith in Christ and not through works prescribed by the law (Romans 3:28). James responds here to people who are claiming to have faith with the implication that they do not need to do works.

James points out that people are justified by works and not by faith alone (v. 24). He states that a faith which does nothing to help the naked and starving but offers only platitudes is dead (vv. 15–17). Any living faith produces works. He follows up this common-sense reasoning with a shocking but logical argument. If faith is merely belief, then demons have faith (v. 19). To make this argument James chooses the most sacred of all traditional beliefs: that the Lord God is one (Deuteronomy 6:4). By pointing out that demons believe God is one, he emphasises that faith cannot simply be a matter of belief. He adds to this argument the comment that the demons 'believe—and shudder' (v. 19). They know their destiny on judgement day. James reminds his fellow Christians throughout this letter that God will judge, and he suggests we prepare for this seriously (for example, 2:13; 3:1; 4:12; 5:8).

James's comment on faith has caused no small controversy in the church as it has been read as a contradiction of the Pauline gospel of salvation. However, James's understanding of faith may be closer to Paul's than we sometimes realise. Paul also tells quarrelling Christians they will stand before the judgement seat of Christ (Romans 14:10; 2 Corinthians 5:10). Paul believes that those justified by faith have God's love poured into their hearts by the Holy Spirit (Romans 5:1–5), and that love fulfils the law (Romans 13:8–10) right to the point of feeding not simply the hungry but even our enemies (Romans 12:20). It seems Paul would be right at home with the idea that we are not saved by faith alone if that means faith is divorced from God's love flowing into us and then out of us in genuine acts of compassion.

5 Humble yourselves

James 4:1–12

Visions of reversal seem to permeate the human imagination. In Western religious and political philosophies of the last couple of centuries, we have developed visions of ourselves as victims who need rescuing. We picture some other person or organisation or situation (for example, the free market, 'the system', political correctness or global warming) as the power that needs to be overthrown or tackled in order that the world can be truly free. Often in these scenarios we imagine ourselves as victims. This may be true for some of us some of the time, and it is never right to minimise or dismiss suffering. However, most of us are far less likely to envisage ourselves as the oppressors or the problem—even though recognising this might be the first step in finding a solution. For example, we are more likely to ask what governments and corporations are doing about global warming than to use our cars less.

This is nothing new. James deals with exactly the same attitudes in his congregation. Jews in the first century AD believed themselves to be victims of Roman imperial oppression and other injustices. They produced visions of Rome overthrown and Palestine living in religious and political liberty. As they heard the words of Jesus (see Matthew 23:12; Luke 6:25), they would have identified Rome as the powerful needing humbling, and themselves as the mourning poor needing exaltation.

James teaches them to take a long, hard look at themselves. When he instructs them to 'lament and mourn and weep' (v. 9), he picks up on Jesus' words in Luke 6:25, but suggests to his audience that they are the oppressors. When he tells them to humble themselves (v. 10), he picks up on Jesus' words in Matthew 23:12, telling his audience they are not victims. He has pointed out the ways they oppress others earlier in the letter. He unmasks their victim illusions and instructs them to take responsibility and get right with God.

However, this is a vision of grace. The oppressors can win as well as the oppressed. Repenting of our misuse of power, wealth and privilege and changing our behaviour counts as an appropriate response to James's command to 'humble yourselves' (v. 10)—and when we do this (as Zacchaeus did in Luke 19:8–9), Jesus will exalt us (v. 10).

6 Pause for thought

James 5:1–18

Few people today would worry about James's teaching on taking oaths (v. 12)—apart from, possibly, those who are asked to take oaths in a court of law or oaths of allegiance. So the 39th article of *The Book of Common Prayer* explicitly interprets James as not banning oaths taken before a magistrate. The idea that we ought to say what we mean is embedded within our culture even if sometimes it is more honoured in the breach than in the observance.

Things were different in the early church. John of Patmos saw an angel swear by God in his vision (Revelation 10:5–6). Paul frequently calls on God as his witness (Romans 1:9; 2 Corinthians 1:23; Galatians 1:20; Philippians 1:8) when wanting to emphasise a point to his congregations. This habit was so deeply ingrained that church leaders—even apostles—were using oaths.

This would have put James in an interesting position. His fellow ministers, even leading ministers of the church, were happy to use oaths in their teaching. However, the words of Jesus (Matthew 5:33–37), on a plain reading, ban the use of oaths entirely. Perhaps that is why James says, at the start of verse 12, 'Above all…' Maybe he makes the point forcefully precisely because he knows church culture is so deeply imbued with the opposite values to those of Jesus on this issue.

Few if any generations of the church have lived in a culture that agreed on every point with Jesus. Many of us Christians, including church leaders, joyfully adopt the values of our age despite the teaching of Jesus. Where we need excuses, we have become remarkably adept at finding them. However, James refuses to give in. In fact, he addresses such issues with a directness that many today would find embarrassing. He points out to the rich that they have laid up treasure for the last days (recalling Jesus' saying in Matthew 6:19–21), but draws attention to the fact that, ironically, this is the wrong kind of treasure and will act as 'evidence against' them when they are judged on the final day (vv. 2–3). Then he turns to the congregation at large and encourages them to remain strong until the Lord Jesus comes to judge (vv. 7–11). Given Jesus will punish the rich and in his compassion and mercy rescue the oppressed, this must have been a letter that split the church down the middle. James can see the difficulties, as he counsels the church not to grumble against each other (presumably the poor against the rich) as such grumbling will incur judgement.

Guidelines

The theme tune to the (now rather old) film *Pretty Woman* claimed 'what was sinful is now complicated'. Culturally we prefer to see ourselves as caught up in situations for which we are not wholly responsible and not to blame. Rather we tend to see ourselves as victims and assume others have responsibility for solving our problems.

James knows this culture well. He challenges his audience to listen hard both to their situation and to the words of Jesus. He will not let them get away with simply identifying themselves as the oppressed who need blessing from God. He instructs them to take a good, hard look at ways in which they oppress others, and he challenges them to change these behaviours. Take some time to think through how you may oppress others and ask what might need to change. If you are short of ideas, check your shopping for unfairly traded goods, or think about how you treat anyone you employ or supervise. Do you treat everyone with equal respect? Do you give as Jesus taught (Matthew 23:23)?

Contemporary churches are often trying to make sense of the gospel in a changing culture that is increasingly intolerant of any absolute religious claim. We are rediscovering what it is to have a marginalised and minority voice—a voice the earliest Christians knew well as it was the only one with which they could speak. James encourages us not to let go of any of Jesus' words as we find our new voice, but to find a greater commitment to living them out.

This is tricky and will throw up thorny issues. However, Jesus taught that through obedience we might learn and find life. Sometimes this involves difficult challenges but, to paraphrase James, if we can find our way out of sinful patterns of behaviour and into obedience to Jesus, we 'will cover a multitude of sins' (5:20).

FURTHER READING

Dale Allison, *James* (Bloomsbury, 2013).

Patrick Hartin, *James* (Liturgical Press, 2003).

Luke Johnson, *The Letter of James* (Doubleday, 1995).

1, 2 and 3 John

Almost at the end of the New Testament we find three letters ascribed to 'John'. None of them is signed in any way other than by superscriptions such as 'the elder', but ancient church tradition ascribes the first at least, together with Revelation, to John the apostle and evangelist. Even in ancient times there was some doubt about whether 2 and 3 John were by the same hand, with some preferring to assign one or both to a second writer, 'John the Presbyter'. Whatever their authorship most scholars agree that they belong to a time towards the end of the first century when the early fellowships in Asia Minor were firmly established. Tradition associates John the evangelist with the church at Ephesus, where, according to Eusebius, John lived into old age 'in Trajan's time'. Trajan became emperor in AD98, and if we imagine John as a disciple with Jesus at the age of perhaps 15, he would have been about 85 years old at the turn of the century. Such an age is unusual for the time but by no means impossible. What is certain is that the writer of 1 John in particular shares with the writer of John's Gospel a deep understanding of the person and ministry of Christ. It is not hard to imagine a godly man reflecting over many years upon the experiences he had travelling around Palestine following his teacher, Jesus.

Drawing deeply on Jewish heritage as well as being rooted in the world of Greco-Roman philosophy, the writing is deeply personal, whether to the churches in general (1 and 2 John) or to a particular friend (3 John). 1 John shares with John's Gospel a sense of the eyewitness, the teenager who marvelled at miracles, drank in deep teaching and stood transfixed before his transfigured and then crucified Lord. At the end of his Gospel John tells us 'his testimony is true'. The similarities in imagery between this Gospel and 1 John in particular give us confidence that this same hand is at work in the letter, and that John invites us to stand together with him beside his and our rabbi.

Quotations are taken from the New Revised Standard Version of the Bible.

1 The Word of life

1 John 1:1–4

John opens with a declaration. He is concerned to establish two things right from the outset. The first is the nature of the Christ he proclaims and the second is his right to make that proclamation. In these opening verses he locates the person of Christ at the very centre of his message and of the life of the church.

Echoing the start of his Gospel, John begins by reminding us of the eternal nature of Christ, that which 'was from the beginning' (v. 1), identifying this eternal Word as the Word of life. We are at once reminded of John 17:3: 'This is eternal life, that they may know you, the only true God, and Jesus Christ whom you have sent.' But this is no remote, theoretical exposition of an unattainable God. For John the outcome of this realisation is to be in fellowship, with God and with his Christian brothers and sisters in the churches. We shall find fellowship in Christ through the love of God to be at the very heart of this letter.

John's declaration is based upon personal experience, 'what we have heard, what we have seen with our eyes, what we have looked at and touched with our hands' (v. 1). The force of these statements is less apparent in English than in the original Greek. John could have written 'what we heard, saw, looked at and touched' as a simple reference to past events which he witnessed in Palestine many years earlier. Instead, 'hear', 'see', 'look' and 'touch' are all in the perfect tense, which in Greek describes something that happened in the past, the effects of which remain with us in the present. So we might understand that for John it is not just the events of the past that are important but the continuing fellowship with Christ, in which he urges us all to join him. Jesus is no longer present with John as he was in Palestine but it seems that for John he can be heard, seen and encountered in the present.

2 Walking in the light and doing truth

1 John 1:5–10

In 1946 a Bedouin shepherd discovered a cache of first-century AD scrolls in a cave on the West Bank. Among the documents in what proved to be the library of the Qumran community was the Community Rule. This document speaks of there being two ways, a way of life and a way of death; a way of light and a way of darkness. This theme is not uncommon in first to early-second-century Judeo-Christian literature. John, however, has new things to say about this teaching: 'God is light and in him there is no darkness at all'. This statement lies at the heart of John's Gospel (John 1:5–9; 3:19–21; 8:12) and it is a very different expression of the gospel from that of Matthew's 'great commission' or Paul's 'justification by faith'. Where Matthew emphasises the coming kingdom and the importance of sharing that news, and Paul focuses upon the significance of faith for the believer, John speaks to us about Christ and his ministry and how that is worked out in our lives.

John first reminds us of the purity of God—'in him there is no darkness' (v. 5). We can only share fellowship with God if we open our lives to that godly light. If we persist in walking the path of darkness then our fellowship with God and one another is built on a lie. Worse still, if we claim to be free from shortcomings we make God a liar.

Echoes of John's Gospel are all around us in these verses: 'I am the way, and the truth, and the life' (John 14:6). For John this way of light is the way of Christ and to walk in the light is to walk in his footsteps. That Christ is the truth is not enough for John. He wants more than an abstract concept of truth or the absence of falsehood. For John, truth is something that must be 'done' rather than asserted. In other words, truth is something we must enact rather than simply marvelling at its beauty from a safe distance. This is a deeply incarnational expression of the gospel which requires us to be absolutely honest in our dealings with God and one another. Perhaps most importantly, it is as we venture out along the way of light and truth that we are ourselves cleansed.

3 Advocate of mercy

1 John 2:1–6

When I was a small choir boy, the parish church I attended celebrated communion only once a month at the main Sunday morning service. In *The Book of Common Prayer* 1662 communion service the prayer of consecration is preceded by the confession, and sandwiched between the two are the 'comfortable words'. These short quotations from scripture reassure the penitent of forgiveness and end with these words based on verses 1–2: 'If any man sin we have an Advocate with the Father, Jesus Christ the righteous, and he is the propitiation for our sins.'

As an eight-year-old chorister, I found that this text held some problems for me. Sin, I thought I might know something about—there had been the unfortunate incident with the glue pot which had led to expulsion from Sunday school and so indirectly accounted for my presence in the choir stalls. Nevertheless I had a suspicion that what God meant by sin might not be exactly the sort of thing I had in mind. Then there was the 'advocate'. Some years were to elapse before I grasped the idea of the friend who stands up to speak for me and pleads my case before the bench. Propitiation? Well, the NRSV has 'atoning sacrifice' (v. 2) but I am not quite sure that does it either. The original word is *hilasmos*, and the best definition for it I have encountered is 'what takes place at the *hilasterion*—the mercy seat'. Christ is the means by which we are shown mercy. And not just us but the whole world—actually all creation.

How does this work? Well, he cleanses us from sin. How does he do that? By walking in the light and inviting us to join him. How do we know if we are truly walking in the light? When we find we are keeping his commandments and being conformed to his example. And then something truly wonderful happens: as we obey him, the love of God is made complete in us. We shall return to the love of God a little later in these notes but for now John wants us to realise that simply claiming we are in Christ is of no account unless we 'walk just as he walked' (v. 6). To be truly part of God's kingdom we must not just talk the talk but walk the walk.

4 An old commandment

Many of John's readers would have either considered themselves to be Jews or at least had significant contact with the local synagogue. They could be expected to know the great commandments to Israel: 'Hear, O Israel: the Lord is our God, the Lord alone. You shall love the Lord your God with all your heart, and with all your soul, and with all your might' (Deuteronomy 6:4–5), and 'you shall love your neighbour as yourself' (Leviticus 19:18). Jesus himself reinforces this teaching in Matthew 22:37, Mark 12:29 and Luke 10:27. John's readers might also have been able to recall that the verse before Leviticus 19:18 begins 'You shall not hate in your heart…' John takes this teaching and weaves it into his own teaching of the two ways of light and darkness. Light, he says, is incompatible with hate for it is those who love that remain in the light.

But he goes further. Not only does walking in the light benefit the disciple, but they in turn benefit the rest of the community because they are not a 'cause for stumbling' (v. 10). The image here is perhaps a little more dramatic than we might imagine. The 'cause for stumbling' was a *skandalon*, a large stone placed in the sand at the centre of a Roman wrestling ring. The task was to upset your opponent by using the *skandalon* to trip them up, allowing you to throw them to the ground. For John, the disciple who allows hate for another to take hold of him is actively contributing to another's downfall and as such 'walks in the darkness' (v. 11).

Using what was probably a well-known hymn John reminds his readers that their sins are forgiven, they know the Father and they have been victorious over evil. John now returns to his theme of love by making sure we understand it is not just love but the object of love that matters. Do not, he urges, love the 'things in the world' (v. 15). The person who values these does not love the Father. This, he reminds us, is foolish because the world and the things that are important to it are transient, whereas the person who does what God wants remains forever. Why do they remain forever? Because they know the Father (John 17:3).

5 Warning against antichrists

We all like a confrontation between good and evil. It's a bit like the cinema: we can hiss at the baddie and cheer for the goody. But casting complex, real-life people as such polarised characters is a lot more difficult than it looks. In the first place, we are prone to assuming we are always on the side of the good and true; yet here, John's warning is not about opposition from beyond the church but from members of the church community who are now preaching a different gospel. We can speculate about what this preaching may have been but all we know for sure is it seems to have been denying Jesus is the Christ. In doing this the preachers deny not just the Son but the Father who sent him.

John is unequivocal in his understanding that it is only in knowing the Son that we can know the Father, and so the Father cannot be truly known apart from the Son. This core truth sets Christianity apart from other faiths. It is not hard to have conversations with other faiths about God, but when we try to talk of Christ as the Son of God it becomes much harder to find a common understanding. But this is our good news, the gospel we 'heard from the beginning' (v. 24) which lives in each one of us. By confessing our trust in the Son we too are 'in the Father' as are all who profess faith in Christ as the Son of the Father.

For John, to know Christ is to know God. Moreover, just as Christ was baptised into a ministry that revealed the deep love of God for the world, so too are we. This is our calling: to reveal God to the world through the pattern of Jesus. We need no other example if we are conformed to Christ. What does this ministry look like? 'He has anointed me to bring good news to the poor. He has sent me to proclaim release to the captives and recovery of sight to the blind, to let the oppressed go free' (Luke 4:18). If we can do these things we shall have nothing to be ashamed of when we, at the last, stand before him.

6 Children of God

1 John 2:29—3:10

Once again we find echoes in today's passage of John's Gospel, particularly the encounter between Jesus and Nicodemus in chapter 3. John uses the same concept of being born anew to describe the reality of a life lived according to the pattern of Christ. We are encouraged to recognise Christlike qualities when we encounter them in people; 'everyone who does right has been born of him' (2:29). This is something to celebrate, but for John it is a celebration of the love of God which is revealed in this way of living: 'See what love the Father has given us' (3:1). Just as in John 3:16, 'For God *so* loved the world…' (my italics), the emphasis here is not so much on the quantity of God's love, inexhaustible though it is, but upon its nature. Our translations rightly preserve the ambiguity of 1 John 3:1, but we could reasonably paraphrase it as 'Just look at the kind of love the Father has given us.'

It is by this love that we are called children of God. We are enfolded in God's love for us and at the same time pouring out that same love into the world. And this is why the world does not understand. The ancient world was in many ways little different from our own. Human beings are much the same nowadays after all. Then, as now, there was no such thing as a free lunch. John's secular contemporaries struggled to understand what these Christians had done to earn themselves such an assurance. Without knowing God in Christ it simply does not make sense.

We have been set a challenging target, that of following in the footsteps of Jesus. There will be times when we fall short of the Father's hopes for us, just as others have before us, but we have the assurance in Christ that God's grace is sufficient for us. Should we lose our way, we serve another master. John calls him the devil but the word originally meant 'slanderer' or 'deceiver', a person in whom there is no truth. When we are walking after Christ in the way of light, truth and love, we too are seen to be doing things that delight God, and by that we are seen to be children of God.

Guidelines

For John the core of who we are as Christians is in being set right with God. John, in common with the writer of Hebrews, uses the image of the blood offering from a sacrifice as the agent of cleansing and redemption (1 John 1:7). This may feel very Old Testament but we need to remember that, for the Hebrews, blood represented life. The value of the sacrifice is not so much the blood spilt as the life offered. Our cleansing is through the life of Christ, whose pattern we adopt as we follow his way. In doing so, we are made clean—not by our own faith but by the faithfulness of Christ.

Not only are we redeemed in the life of Christ but we are also God's agents, seeking to live a godly life and learning to recognise Christ in the bustle of a busy day, with its chance encounters and conversations, and to reflect his life into the world around us. How can we do this? By loving God and walking in the light of Christ, and so coming to know the Father—in knowing whom we have eternal life.

11–17 April

1 Love one another

1 John 3:11—4:6

To love one another is nothing if not challenging. Having explained that it is through the love of God that we are called God's children, John now grounds this teaching very firmly in reality. To love God and be loved by him is wonderful, but if we do not show that same love to the other members of our fellowship it is worth very little. The measure of our standing with God is in the way we treat those around us: 'We know that we have passed from death to life because we love one another' (3:14). If we cannot find love for others but harbour resentment for them or refuse to share our wealth with the needy, we are no better than murderers who have refused the gift of life in Christ.

Once again we are challenged: don't just talk about it, do something!

The concept of 'doing truth' returns. But there is comfort should we become fearful that we have not fulfilled God's hopes for us, because 'God is greater than our hearts' (3:20). (In Greek and Hebrew thought the heart is more the seat of understanding than of the emotions.) This is good to reflect upon during times when it seems we shall never be able to live up to the example of Christ. We are doing truth when we follow Christ's commandments, acknowledging his authority and model and working out his example in our love for one another. Since we have 'the Spirit of God' (v. 2) we can be confident that he is with us.

How can we be sure the spirit we encounter is from God? John returns to the centrality of Christ as the pattern for the Father's love: 'every spirit that confesses that Jesus Christ has come in the flesh is from God' (4:2). There once again is the irreducible touchstone of our faith. In the final analysis Sunday school was right—the answer is always 'Jesus'. Do the things we are hearing or seeing in the world around us fit the character of the Christ we know? The secular world is not conformed to Christ; it wasn't in John's time and it isn't now. Perhaps a more important question is whether the truth we are speaking and doing is one that Jesus would own.

2 God is love

1 John 4:7–19

We are all a little prone to thinking in stereotypes, and quite often those stereotypes are based upon caricatures. That is certainly the case with much of the polemic directed against the church by proponents of the new atheism. Often we are left wondering how to answer charges that have little basis in the reality of the God we know. In these verses John gives us a brief character sketch of his God. The Jews had a healthy respect for the presence of God. The high priest would venture into the Holy of Holies in the temple only on the Day of Atonement, and on that day he was attached to a cord by which his body could be drawn back to safety were the unthinkable to occur. But the God John knows is a very different character. Awesome? Certainly. Frightening? No.

'God,' John tells us, 'is love' (v. 8). And this God is revealed in the gift of Christ who showed God's love to us that we might live through that same love. The initiative rests firmly with God. 'We love because he first loved us' (v. 19) and it is in our love for others that God's love is perfected in us. How can this be? It seems that the perfection/fulfilment of love is in the love returned to the lover by the beloved, shown in our love for one another. Such love must be freely offered, without caveat or any attempt to control the beloved. It is an enormous risk. The outcome is in the hands of the beloved. Perhaps this is what 'playing God' is really like. For God to be who he is he must take the risk of loving us, meaning he cannot allow himself to control the outcome. If he does, the outcome is false and becomes meaningless.

The implications of this are truly enormous. This is no arrogant deity demanding obedience and conformity, but rather the loving Father who bears with his children's shortcomings, always ready to forgive, never imposing but simply questioning if we lack anything. This is the pattern that became incarnate in Christ and the image to which we are being conformed as we seek to work out our calling in Christ in the world.

3 Faith's victory in proclaiming the Son

1 John 4:20—5:12

John returns to the idea that truth is of God, and anything that is not truth has no place in God. He restates the essential truth that it is not sufficient to claim to love God if there is no evidence of love for other church members. This teaching is reinforced by reference to 'the commandment' (4:21), surely a reflection of John's Gospel: 'This is my commandment, that you love one another as I have loved you' (John 15:12).

John draws again on the 'born anew' imagery also found in his Gospel. He establishes that the principle characteristic of one who has been 'born of God' is belief that Jesus is indeed the Christ. It is not possible in John's eyes for love of God not to include the recognition of Jesus as the Christ and as the Son of God. There are responsibilities too: we must strive to keep the commandments of God, for that is what loving God means. By our trust in the life and ministry of Jesus we too shall overcome the world, as we walk the way he walked, seeking always to be conformed to his example.

1 John 5:6 has puzzled theologians for almost 2000 years. Some regard the references to water and blood as indicating the beginning and end of the ministry of Christ. Others emphasise the outcome of that ministry, remembering 1:7: 'the blood of Jesus his Son cleanses us from all sin'. A third interpretation is that water and blood refer to the rites of the church in baptism and communion. Perhaps John is drawing together the experience of the church in baptism, communion and the indwelling of the Spirit to demonstrate that these three all testify to Christ. Any teaching that does not have Christ at the centre of God's work leads not to truth and life but to falsehood and death.

Those who believe the testimony about Jesus know God because they have glimpsed the immensity of God's love incarnate in Jesus. It is the church's calling and, therefore, our calling to trust that the revelation of the love of God in Christ is true, and to reflect that love to the world in all that we say and do. I fear I am repeating myself but I think John is too!

4 The knowledge of eternal life

1 John 5:13–21

John began his letter with a declaration: 'we… declare to you the eternal life that was with the Father' (1:2). He now draws it to a close with a restatement of why he is writing: 'I write these things to you who believe in the name of the Son of God, so that you may know that you have eternal life' (v. 13). Throughout the letter John has emphasised the centrality of Christ as the Son of God, by whom we can know the Father, 'in knowledge of whom is eternal life' (Second Collect for Peace at Matins, *The Book of Common Prayer*).

Given our knowledge of God in the example of Christ, John encourages us to be bold in prayer; those who know God may make their petitions with confidence knowing them to be in accordance with the Father's love for us (see John 14:13–14). We are encouraged to pray for one another should we fall short of God's expectations for us and have confidence that such prayer will restore us. Many have speculated about the 'sin that is mortal' (v. 16). This sits uncomfortably with the great assurances in the earlier chapters, but we might understand it as simply descriptive. Since Christ is the means by which we know the Father and so share eternal life, if we refuse to recognise the Son of God we cannot know God and so we cannot share in his life. Once again we encounter the risk of love. God in Christ has given all to bring us into a proper relationship with him. But he leaves us free to walk away if we choose. He cannot compel, only invite.

John concludes with three great affirmations: we know those who are reborn of God do not continue in sin; we know we are God's children; and we know the Son of God has come and shown us the true God. Throughout this letter the core of John's message has been the person and practice of Christ. His insistence on this focus suggests there were perhaps other messages being proclaimed among the churches. John's message for us is to ensure our focus remains upon Jesus. Anything contrary to this is not of God. Beware of imitations!

5 The elect lady

2 John

The author of 2 John is identified as 'the elder'. Tradition considers him to have been either John the evangelist or another John the elder. He writes to 'the elect lady'. This may have been a Christian woman with a family but it is perhaps more likely that 'the elect lady' represents the church. This imagery is common in other Christian writings in the early second century. It is analogous to the custom in the Greco-Roman world of giving abstract concepts such as cities or regions a human, usually female, identity. The elect lady, then, represents the church community to whom the elder is writing. The members of that church are her children.

Who is the elder? By what authority does he write? Whom does he represent? In the final verse he writes, 'The children of your elect sister send you their greetings' (v. 13). It seems he is writing on behalf of another church fellowship and has its authority to write to another church.

The writer is clearly concerned that there are others travelling among the churches who are proclaiming a different gospel. As in 1 John the key message here is the importance of the confession that Jesus the Christ was incarnate in Palestine and walked among men and women, teaching, releasing and healing. Only with this understanding is it possible for the believer to enjoy a proper relationship with God the Father.

Once again, we are encouraged to be 'walking in the truth' (v. 4). And there is another aspect of truth we might consider. The Greek word for truth covers rather more than our English word. *Alētheia* is not just an abstract ideal but also has a sense of 'what is truly real'. It is related to the name of the mythological River Lēthe, the river of forgetfulness, but carries the negating 'a-' prefix. Truth is something so real that it is absolutely unforgettable.

These early churches see themselves as very much part of a greater Church. They know they need one another and the proclamation and safeguarding of the gospel is a task they all share. Our fragmented 21st-century churches need to hear this. We need one another. Just as individual Christians cannot abandon the church, individual churches cannot abandon Christendom. We are in this together and how we work that out is a measure of how well we have understood our gospel.

6 Dealing with dissension

3 John

The third letter of John is also from 'the elder'. It is addressed to Gaius, a man clearly well known to and respected by the writer. The content deals with matters of church governance and the concept of 'walking in the truth' (v. 4) is once again found. However 3 John has a much more personal touch. The writer enquires after the health of his friend, bodily and spiritual. Such an opening is more typical of the personal-letter-writing genre of the ancient world than other New Testament letters. Whether a letter from Gaius arrived with 'the friends' (vv. 3, 5, 10, 15) is not clear, but this letter is a response to news from another church. There is a pastoral relationship between Gaius and the writer, who describes Gaius as one of his 'children' (v. 4), and the writer's joy in hearing that Gaius has remained faithful to the truth of the gospel is evident. Gaius is encouraged to maintain his care for fellow workers in the gospel whether previously known to him or not.

It seems this is not the first letter the elder has written to Gaius's church. A previous letter to a self-appointed elder has not been acknowledged (v. 9). Gaius has perhaps asked the writer to come and visit his church in the hope that the writer's authority will be sufficient to correct the abuses that are taking place. The charges against Diotrephes appear to be spreading slander of others, refusing the hospitality of the church to 'the friends', and even expelling those who oppose him in this from the fellowship. All is not lost, however. Gaius is encouraged to imitate what is good and another man, Demetrius, is commended as a suitable example.

Dealing with dissension is never easy but in verse 11 the elder lays down a simple guideline: 'do not imitate what is evil but imitate what is good'. The temptation to respond in kind when challenged is exactly that—an imitation of evil. The examples we must seek out are those of men and women like Demetrius about whom 'everyone has testified favourably' (v. 12), and not only everyone but the truth itself. How can we know if the truth testifies? Well, if Jesus is the way, the truth and the life then we can expect to see reflections of his pattern in those who claim to act in his name.

Guidelines

A common question asked of Christians is 'If God is almighty why does he permit suffering?' One response is that he must, because he is love. And this is the love we see in Christ, showing us the way to the Father and opening to us the Father's heart of love; pleading our cause before God, sharing our suffering, and, just possibly, atoning for love's hazard. There is no fear in this kind of love, only the deep joy of love made perfect in its imitation, as love sacrifices all in atonement for the failings of a creation given the freedom to love.

There are two ways. One, the way of the world, is focused on self and conforms to the expectations of the world. It leads to death. The other is a radical path that eschews violence and sets self aside; it is the way Christ has shown us in his life. The world does not understand this way because it has not recognised the love of God in Christ. Yet this path leads to victory over the world and it is this path we are called to tread, towards the knowledge of God that is eternal life. This is what it is to walk in the light.

'By this everyone will know that you are my disciples, if you have love for one another' (John 13:35). If we wonder why the world finds our churches irrelevant this may give us a clue. The thing that drew men and women to the early church was, more than anything else, the love they showed to the world in their care for their people. Love attracts, and in the end, love is all we have to offer.

FURTHER READING

C.A. Eberhart, 'Characteristics of Sacrificial Metaphors' in G. Gelardini (ed.), *Hebrews: Contemporary Methods—New Insights* (Brill, 2005).

A. Stewart, *On the Two Ways: Life or Death, Light or Darkness: Foundational texts in the tradition* (St Vladimir's Seminary Press, 2011).

A. Stewart, *The Original Bishops: Office and order in the first Christian communities* (Baker Academic, 2014).

W.H. Vanstone, *Love's Endeavour, Love's Expense* (DLT, 1977, 2007).

Remember me: faith and dementia

Mary died recently. She had advanced dementia and was living in a care home. She was frail and her communication skills were limited. Faith commitment had not been part of her story, but she often spoke anxiously in those last days of how unworthy she felt of God's love and forgiveness. The chaplain reassured her of God's gift of these, and gave her a simple cross to hold to remind her of Jesus. A couple of weeks after that, no longer able to speak, she died, determinedly reaching for, then holding on to, that cross. Surely, as Jesus said to the woman in the crowd who reached out to touch him, 'Daughter, your faith has healed you. Go in peace' (Mark 5:34).

There are currently around 850,000 people living in the UK with dementia. That number is predicted to rise to over two million by the middle of this century. It's an issue that affects us all—and it raises many questions for biblical faith and our understanding of what God is doing in the lives of people affected by this disease. But people with dementia are not a separate kind of being! Like anyone else they are made in God's image and loved by him. Before God, we are equal. In this series, we'll be reflecting on what we might learn from those directly affected by dementia and how that illuminates our own understanding of faith.

Our Bible readings will help us consider issues such as identity, the grace of dependence, the importance of belonging and more—significantly, not only for those facing the challenges of dementia (or another disability, or age), but for all of us, whatever our situation. As we reflect on the devastating effects of dementia, it raises questions—and brings light—for our own being with God.

'... neither death nor life, neither angels nor demons, neither the present nor the future, nor any powers, neither height nor depth, nor anything else in all creation, will be able to separate us from the love of God that is in Christ Jesus our Lord' (Romans 8:38–39).

Quotations are taken from the New International Version of the Bible.

1 Do this in remembrance of me

Luke 22:7–20

Memory is a paradox for those with dementia; stories of times past fund awareness of the present moment. For all of us, personal stories celebrate who we are, and bring security for whatever lies ahead. For all of us, too, whether or not our memory is failing, rituals of the past can bring a sense of God's presence in the now. Memory of our shared story is the God-given silver thread running through the Bible and into eternity. In Luke 22 the Passover feast converges with the new-covenant revelation of a feast of remembrance that reminds God's people of what he has done, is doing and will do for all his people.

The Passover reminds the disciples of their nation's release from enslavement in Egypt (Exodus 12:1–28). Its unleavened bread and sacrificed lamb (Luke 22:7) have become motifs of God's gift of salvation, celebrated each year, especially at significant times of renewal, such as the return from exile (Ezra 6:19–22). The lamb, given for the cleansing of God's people, was always a reminder of the gift of his forgiveness. Prophetically, as in Isaiah 53, it pointed, mysteriously to the coming Messiah who would save his people. In Luke 22, Jesus shows the disciples dramatically that *he* is the fulfilment of God's promises (vv. 17–20)—the lamb to be sacrificed for our sin, the body broken, the blood shed. 'Do this in remembrance of me' (v. 19) he commands, pointing forwards to the future life of the church, and to the messianic banquet (v. 18) in the coming kingdom.

This 'feast', with its familiar words and actions, helps to trigger awareness in the present. It also reminds us that we come as equals to the Lord's table—each one of us needing God's forgiveness and grace. It's a time when we serve one another. Notice, it is the most prominent of the disciples who do the work of preparation (v. 8). The symbols of bread and wine remind us—through taste, smell and touch—of the story of what God in Jesus has done for us. This is a feast for all, as together, as his saved people, we remember Jesus. It is also for the individual, whoever we are—a moment when God uses memory to bring awareness of his own love and forgiveness for each one of us.

2 Who am I?

Psalm 139

'She's not the same person,' says the grieving relative of a loved one living with dementia. The painful words raise a question we may have asked of ourselves: 'Who am I?' Here, in his own desperate times, the author of Psalm 139 discovers a sense of identity and security grounded in the wisdom and love of almighty God. The important question perhaps is not so much 'Who am I?' but 'Who is this God who knows us, chose to make us, and surrounds us with his love?'

He is omniscient (vv. 1–6). God knows everything about me—my thoughts, my words, my actions. The psalmist finds his burden lifted as he acknowledges before the all-knowing God his vulnerability. His eyes are raised from difficult circumstances to notice that this loving God surrounds him. For the forgiven sinner, who knows his weakness, there is only rest and hope as we realise this powerful God is on our side. He hems us in with his loving presence, behind and ahead (v. 5). He knows it all; he knows *me*.

He is omnipresent (vv. 7–12). We may feel that we, or others we love, are lost in deepest darkness. But we—and they—cannot be lost from God. He holds us fast whatever our situation (vv. 9–10). And strangely, we sometimes find God's light shining more clearly in the dark times (vv. 11–12).

God knows who we are (vv. 13–18). Here, the psalmist worships his creator, who designed and made each human being. He has known every person from before they were born and through every moment of their lives—to this day, and beyond (v. 16). Whoever we are, loved or unloved by others, we are precious to God, secure in his countless loving thoughts (vv. 17–18).

God is our beginning and our end (vv. 19–24). Our identity is founded in God's loving care and purpose. This can prompt us to pray for ourselves and for those who may have forgotten who they are—

knowing that we, and they, are safe in our Father's love: 'Search me, God, and know my heart... lead me in the way everlasting' (vv. 23, 24).

3 The grace of dependence

Mark 2:1–12

'I don't want to be a burden,' says our elderly, sick relative. Yet our mutual burdensomeness, as John Stott has pointed out, is part of God's design for us (Galatians 6:2). As the incarnate Christ submitted to 'the dignity of dependence', so must we (Stott, 'The age of dependence', *Christianity*, January 2010). In today's reading we're shown the saving grace of a man's dependence on his friends.

Those with dementia (or the elderly, or those with other difficulties) can often find themselves excluded. They may easily be forgotten, or things may just be too difficult for others to organise. So it could have been for the paralysed man in today's reading. The crowds came to hear Jesus preach and 'there was no room left' (v. 2). Cue the man's friends! Their practical action, determination, courage, love for their friend and awareness of his worth bring them all to Jesus (vv. 3–4). The man accepts his dependence, and it leads to much more than physical healing (v. 5). (Who knows what transformation this event brought to his friends?)

Jesus first responds to the friends' faith, exercised on another's behalf (v. 5). Sometimes, we are beyond having faith ourselves—and, whether we know it or not, we need to be carried by others to Jesus and laid at his feet. Jesus' first words are surprising: 'Son, your sins are forgiven' (v. 5). For the religious leaders, these are shocking, blasphemous words (vv. 6–7). But Jesus knows the priority for this man: peace with God—and, yes, Jesus is indeed God (v. 7).

The friends had brought this man for healing; Jesus gives him much more! Forgiveness of sins had eternal significance, and the healing of his earthly body would bring transformation to his life on earth (v. 12). The paralysed man's acceptance of his dependence brought the good news and truth of Christ to his friends, the religious leaders and the crowds, who end up praising God (v. 12).

Sometimes we are called to dependence; sometimes we are those on whom others depend. Whichever is true for us at this point in our lives, we ultimately all depend on Christ, who himself 'lives to intercede' for us (Hebrews 7:25).

4 Included or belonging?

1 Corinthians 12:12–27

When the local church first learnt of Dorothy's dementia, they were sympathetic and helpful. But gradually she seemed to be forgotten. Dorothy (and her husband) felt they were on their own. We may talk of making sure the elderly or disabled are 'included' in our church life, but 'being included' is not the same as 'belonging' (John Swinton, *Dementia: Living in the memories of God*, p. 279). In these Bible verses, Paul talks about what it means to belong to the body of Christ.

Jesus prayed for his followers that 'all of them may be one, Father, just as you are in me and I am in you' (John 17:21). In the mystical unity of the Trinity, there is diversity, yet oneness—and it is our privilege to be caught up in it (vv. 12–14). Through his Spirit, as Christ's body, believers are equipped for his work (vv. 18–20). Whatever our situation, whoever we are—rich or poor, young or old, able or disabled—we stand equal before God, 'baptised by one Spirit' (v. 13). Each of us is necessary for body's well-being (vv. 15–20). Those with dementia, for example, 'belong'—and have a unique role to play. This unity is not about our 'including' them, but rather discovering and honouring what God is doing in our lives together, as we serve him and one another (v. 25).

But we humans have a divisive tendency to honour status. Here, in God's upside-down reality, things are different: 'those parts of the body that seem to be weaker are indispensable' (v. 22); those who seem less important are to be especially honoured (v. 24). Such behaviour characterises the body of Christ (v. 26). And this is not easy. Suffering in one part of the body affects every part. I remember Dorothy, far into her journey with dementia, reaching out to touch my face. 'But how are you?' she asked with concern. So my sister's pain affects me—and, as part of the body, we show concern for each other (v. 26).

5 What if I forget Jesus?

Romans 8:31–39

For some Christians diagnosed with dementia, the possibility of forgetting God brings disturbing questions about our faith. Laura, reflecting on her diagnosis of Alzheimer's disease, wrote, 'I may not remember him, but he will remember me' (quoted in Malcolm Goldsmith, *In a Strange Land… People with dementia and the local church*, p. 133). In today's passage, there is good news for any who fear for their own, or a loved one's, separation from God.

Notice how all the assurances in these verses rest on God's promises and actions. There is nothing we can do—our salvation depends on him; we are 'justified freely by his grace' (Romans 3:24). For people who know they are reaching the end of their earthly life, this is a precious message. As memories from past times surface, there may be a desperate need to put things right with God. In response, God's word tells us 'there is now no condemnation' for those trusting in Christ (Romans 8:1). But what if our condition makes it impossible for us to think about these truths? Christine Bryden writes movingly of the beginning of her journey into dementia, of trusting in the Holy Spirit within her, 'and the fellowship of the Body of Christ around me' (Goldsmith, *In a Strange Land…*, p. 131).

And here, in these verses, there is deeper assurance still. The certainty is that, whatever our circumstances, God himself is on our side (vv. 31, 38–39). While our situation may not change, God's presence and our hope in him can give strength to bring us through 'trouble or hardship' (v. 35), the trials of old age or dementia. More than this, Christ himself is praying for us (v. 34). We may be beyond words or thoughts, yet God knows, and Jesus prays. Through him, 'we are more than conquerors' (v. 37).

These are truths that, like Laura and Christine, we might score into our hearts and minds as we prepare ourselves—and others—for whatever lies ahead on the path God has for us. The glorious litany of impossibility in verses 38 to 39 makes it clear: nothing can—or will be able to—separate us from the love of God (v. 39).

6 Thanks be to God!

1 Corinthians 15:50–58

Bert's body is frail. Slowly he manages to say, 'Jesus died… He rose again!' Then, with tears coming: 'We… will… all… be… changed!' There is no denying the ongoing 'sting' of death and human suffering (v. 55), but for those who know a loving God and victorious Christ, there is hope.

It's a mystery. Every one of us is confined to a perishable body. We may not have dementia or another serious illness, but our time-limited bodies are in decline: this is the nature of our fallen, dusty existence (1 Corinthians 15:44–49). The hope and promise of today's verses is that these failing bodies will be transformed (vv. 51–54). The flaw in the big picture of life is that we and our world have been spoilt by sin (v. 56). We live with the consequences of this during our earthly lives. But praise God! Sin has been dealt with through the Son of God's death on the cross and resurrection (vv. 55–57). We have hope in the present, and continuing transformation lies ahead. 'Fear?' says Bert. 'There is no fear in Jesus!'

For believers, like Bert, who may seem lost in forgetfulness and confusion, it's possible to glimpse the beginning of this transformation, through their faith in the victorious Christ. Scripture readings, familiar hymns and shared prayer may all bring moments of response. Yet, while rejoicing in our Christian hope, it does bring challenge. Many experiencing the awful reality of their perishing bodies are afraid, feeling guilty and without hope. For all of us, there is not much time. Bert knows the truth of verse 58. He talks of praying for his carers. Even at this difficult time of his life, he is sharing his hope in Christ. These verses encourage us personally to rejoice in Christian hope, but also to 'stand firm' and give ourselves 'to the work of the Lord' (v. 58). Could this include sharing the gift of Jesus' love with those who are standing alone, in fear, at the end of life's journey—perhaps through simply being present with them? It won't be 'in vain' (v. 58).

'Thanks be to God! He gives us the victory through our Lord Jesus Christ' (v. 57).

Guidelines

Dementia (or advanced age or disability) brings huge challenges—for mission, for ministry and for our own relationship with God. What is a biblical response?

Further questions to reflect on:

- Thank God for the faith of the elderly and ill who belong to your church. What are you learning from them?
- What happens to our faith if we forget God?
- Are there people in your church with dementia? What more could you do to support them (and their loved ones) in their continuing faith journey?
- Included or belonging? 'Now you are the body of Christ, and each one of you is a part of it' (1 Corinthians 12:27). How is our concern for one another being realised in our life as believers?
- How might you share God's love and hope with those facing dementia in the wider community?

Of course, in the end, it's not about us. Our salvation and hope depend on God: his gift, his grace—and his love.

FURTHER READING

Christine Bryden, *Dancing with Dementia* (JKP, 2005).

Robert Davis, *My Journey into Alzheimer's Disease* (Tyndale House, 1989).

Malcolm Goldsmith, *In a Strange Land... People with dementia and the local church* (4M Publications, 2004).

Benjamin Mast, *Second Forgetting: Remembering the power of the gospel during Alzheimer's disease* (Zondervan, 2014).

John Swinton, *Dementia: Living in the memories of God* (Eerdmans, 2012).

Revelation 1—3

The book of Revelation holds out many challenges, but with them, great rewards.

The first challenge is that we are not very familiar with this kind of writing. We come across something like it in Ezekiel, parts of Daniel and Zechariah in the Old Testament—but we find these texts just as baffling. Jesus uses similar language of cosmic realities in the so-called 'little apocalypse' (Mark 13, Matthew 24 and Luke 21:5–36) and neither is asked for nor offers an explanation. Jesus and his first followers were clearly familiar with the conventions and meaning of this kind of symbolic language, which was common in their world.

The second challenge relates to Revelation's context. Unlike other apocalyptic writing, Revelation is written to a very specific situation—and the details of this are lost to many readers. Although some parts of the book have very general application, other parts (especially the seven messages) make very particular references which John's first readers would have understood easily enough.

The third challenge is found in John's extensive use of the Old Testament. By one reckoning, Revelation alludes to the Old Testament more than 600 times in its 404 verses—once or twice in every verse. Whether this is by design or simply the product of a mind saturated with the scriptures, it means we cannot make sense of John's meaning without knowing the scriptures he is drawing on.

So do the rewards make it worth the effort? Will we learn something here we could not find out elsewhere in the New Testament? At one level, the answer to this should be 'No.' When Revelation was eventually accepted as part of the canon of the New Testament, it was because it was believed to proclaim the same gospel found in other New Testament writings. If anyone suggests there is something different here, we should be suspicious!

And yet Revelation offers us a 'worked example' of what it means to live out the gospel in the context of ideological conflict. Nowhere else is there the same detailed exploration of what it means to be a faithful witness to Jesus in a cultural and ideological context that resists his claims.

And nowhere else is the gospel expressed in such vivid terms which grip our imagination. Increasingly, the contemporary church needs to learn 'how to sing the Lord's song in a strange land' (Psalm 137:4), and there is no better place to start than with this text.

Quotations are taken from the New International Version of the Bible.

1 The revelation of Jesus Christ

Revelation 1

The opening of the book introduces a number of key ideas. This is a 'revelation' (v. 1) (Greek: *apocalypsis*), the only place in 'apocalyptic' literature where this term occurs. It comes from God, but it is centred on the person of Jesus. Although there is angelic mediation, what John witnesses is the 'word of God' and Jesus' own witness—in faithfully testifying, John is following Jesus' example and encouraging his hearers to do the same (vv. 1–2). John clearly envisages that what he has written will be read in the assembled congregations; there is a blessing for the lector, who reads the words aloud, and for all those assembled to listen (v. 3).

John then reverts to a more recognisable greeting in the form of a standard letter opening (vv. 4–5). But the greeting is distinctively trinitarian, being from God (John adapts God's self-designation in Exodus 3:14), from the seven spirits (echoing the sevenfold spirit in Isaiah 11:2), and from Jesus. John then switches to praise of God, a notable feature of Revelation that invites participation from his readers. This praise combines an early Christian idea (being free from sin, Romans 6:7) with Old Testament ideas from Exodus 19:6, Daniel 7:13 and Zechariah 12:10. The final comment of this section, 'I am the Alpha and the Omega' (v. 8), borrows language from Greco-Roman magical cults. John is weaving a rich tapestry from three strands: the Old Testament, his contemporary culture and what God has done in Jesus.

In verse 9 John returns to letter form, and identifies with his readers in their experience of living in 'in-between' times. They have all, on the one hand, encountered the grace of God in the kingdom that Jesus has inaugurated. Yet, on the other hand, they feel the pressure of 'tribulation' (persecution), which is the lot of all who follow Jesus (Mark 10:30; Acts 14:22). And they all require the 'patient endurance' (v. 9) to live through persecution in the light of the kingdom.

The vision John sees of Jesus in verses 12 to 16 combines priestly and angelic motifs with both the 'one like a son of man' from Daniel 7 and the One on the throne that he approaches. This anticipates the fusion of language about the Lamb and the One on the throne in chapters 4 and 5. John sends his letter, the account of his visionary experience, to the seven congregations in the order you would actually visit them by road. This cosmic vision is rooted in the real lives of John's readers.

2 Proclamations from the king

Revelation 2:1–7

Chapters 2 and 3 contain not letters to each congregation (*ekklesia*), since the whole of Revelation is a letter, but royal pronouncements from the one who is 'ruler of the kings of the earth' (1:5). Given the order of revelation in 1:1 (from God to Jesus, to his angel, to John, to the reader and finally to the hearers), 'the angel' in 2:1 is best understood as the one who can communicate God's message to his people. At the beginning of each message, the hearers are reminded of one aspect of the vision of Jesus from chapter 1; the white light of the vision is split, as if by a prism, shining a distinct colour on each community. First, those in Ephesus are reminded that Jesus is the source of their protection and security (he holds the stars) as well as the one who is present with them (he walks among the lampstands).

Ephesus was a centre of wealth and culture, the second city of the empire, with a population of more than 250,000. Its splendid architecture was crowned by the Temple of Artemis, one of the seven wonders of the ancient world. And around this time, Ephesus was awarded the title Guardian of the Imperial Cult. So for Christians, there was both pride and challenge in their city. In this context, the risen Christ has much to commend them for. They are energetic and committed, ready for hard work and living out faith in practical action. Twice they are commended for their 'patient endurance' (vv. 2, 3), that key quality for living faithfully in a hostile world. With that, they are also discerning; they have rejected evildoers, have 'tested all things' (1 Thessalonians 5:20–21; 1 John 4:1) and (in echoes of some of Paul's disputes) have turned from false apostles. They have also rejected the 'Nicolaitans'—probably a term coined by John to designate some problem which is now lost to us.

And yet, while the superstructure of faith is in place, the heart has gone out of it. Duty has extinguished joy; hard work has displaced warm love; perhaps even the things of God are of more interest than God himself. The Ephesians need to rediscover their first love for the one who holds them and walks in their midst if they are to enjoy life in all its fullness.

3 Encouragement and challenge

Revelation 2:8–17

The second message, to Smyrna, offers no rebuke, only encouragement. Jesus speaks as 'the First and the Last' (v. 8), the beginning and end of all things, the one 'who died and came to life again' (v. 8)—just as Smyrna had come back to life when the ruined, ancient city was refounded by Alexander the Great. Jesus not only knows what the church in Smyrna is going through, but has experienced it for himself—he who was rich for our sake became poor (2 Corinthians 8:9).

The language about the Jews reflects serious conflict and oppression for the small Christian community. Smyrna had a large Jewish population, and now that followers of Jesus were mostly separated from the synagogue, they had lost the degree of protection that Romans granted Jews as a *religio licta*, which exempted them from the demands of the imperial cult. Yet Jesus promises this time of trial will be strictly limited ('ten days' (v. 10)), and the rewards for endurance far outshine the cost of faithfulness. The people of Smyrna knew all about crowns; called the 'Crown of Asia', Smyrna vied with Ephesus to be known as first city in the region. It hosted important games, where the winner was awarded a crown, and so had a crown on its coins.

The third message is to the Christians in another important city, modern-day Bergama, who faced challenges from without and within. 'Where Satan has his throne' (v. 13) could allude to the appearance of the hill on which the upper city sits, or the shape of the temple to Zeus that was there (now in the Pergamum Museum in Berlin). But it more likely refers to Pergamum being a regional centre of worship of the emperor, the one who wielded the *ius gladii*, the power of the sword. The challenge here was living in the midst of a culture and an ideology systematically opposed to the claim that Jesus (not Caesar) is Lord. This opposition had led to one death already; we know nothing else of Antipas other than that he was following in the pattern of Jesus by being a 'faithful witness' (Greek: *martyros*, 1:5; 2:13).

Just as the start of the message looks back to the initial vision of Jesus, so the end looks forward to the final visions of the book (the 'second death' occurs in 20:6, 20:14 and 21:8). The best is yet to be!

4 Money talks

Revelation 2:18–29

The longest and most complex of the seven messages is addressed to the city about which we know least, Thyatira. There are few ruins remaining of the ancient city in the middle of the modern town of Akhisar. What we do know is that money mattered in Thyatira. This was one of the first cities to use coins, and as it was not in a strong position militarily, it relied on trade for its prosperity and importance. It was on major trade routes north and south, and in Acts 16:14 Paul meets a cloth trader from the city, named Lydia. With trade came trade guilds—inscriptions mention more guilds in Thyatira than in any other city in the province of Asia—and with trade guilds came guild religions. The guilds were as much religious organisations as they were economic, each having their own gods. To change religious affiliation always had economic consequences, as the Ephesians realised in Acts 19:23–41. So to protect one's prosperity meant a compromise in belief—and a change in belief meant risking one's financial security.

Jezebel, mentioned in verse 20, was the wife of Ahab and arch-enemy of Elijah and Elisha (see 1 Kings 16 to 2 Kings 9). She was never accused of 'sexual immorality', but of leading God's people to worship other gods. We therefore need to read 'sexual immorality' as a metaphor for being unfaithful to God—as used by Hosea and other Old Testament prophets—both here and elsewhere in Revelation. As with the names of other antagonists (Balaam and Nicolaitans), this is most likely a term coined by John for something he sees in the Christian community. Jesus' judgement sounds severe, but needs to be read in the context of Revelation's imagery. His warfare is with the sword of his *mouth* (2:16)—his words of truth—and brings about the death of false claims. To 'strike her children dead' (v. 23) means that 'Jezebel's' following will not last.

To those who have continued in 'love and faith... service and perseverance' (v. 19) nothing more is needed. In an echo of the edict from Acts 15:28, the message makes clear that there are no first- and second-class followers of Jesus. To all who stay faithful, the reward is not only to share in Jesus' authority (v. 26) but to share in Jesus himself, 'the morning star' (v. 28; 22:16).

5 A tale of two cities

Revelation 3:1–13

The next two messages, to the fifth and sixth Christian communities, are in stark contrast to one another—the first contains little praise, while the second contains no rebuke. They are addressed to two contrasting cities as well. Sardis was ancient, prestigious and proud. It had been the seat of Croesus, a king of legendary wealth. And its upper city (acropolis) was so impregnable it had never been taken by force. But it had been taken, not once, but twice, by stealth. The citizens had been so sure of themselves and their fortress that they had posted no night watch. When the enemy noticed someone coming out of a hidden back door, they used that route to take the city while the people slept. Three hundred years later, another enemy read the account—and did the same thing. The people were still complacent and sleeping!

'Wake up!' calls Jesus. Faith is not about resting on your laurels, thinking that your situation (your upbringing, your track record, your reputation) will keep you safe. It is about walking, daily, with Jesus, and heeding his call to holy living, as indeed some have continued to do.

By contrast, Philadelphia was the newest of the seven cities. Like others, it was devastated in an earthquake in AD17—but the people remained fearful and continued to live in the surrounding fields rather than returning to the city itself. In the light of the fear of opposition from Jews who had not received Jesus, Jesus himself reassures them. He has placed before them an 'open door' (v. 8), which usually means an opportunity for mission (1 Corinthians 16:9; 2 Corinthians 2:12; Colossians 4:3); not only will the opposition cease, but the opponents will come to acknowledge Jesus themselves (v. 9)! The language here belongs to the polemical debate about who was the true Jew—one with the outward marks of Judaism, or one who listened to God's revelation of himself in Jesus (compare Romans 2, especially verse 29). As the language of the weak (the Christians) in the face of the strong (the Jews), it offers words of protest; if used as the language of the strong (Christendom) against the weak (Judaism), it becomes a word of oppression.

As the Philadelphian Christians hold on to God, God will hold on to them; whatever threatens to shake them, God will make them an unshakeable part of his temple, where he himself takes up residence.

6 Taking the temperature

Revelation 3:14–22

This message is perhaps the best-known of the seven—and the most misinterpreted! In our own context, being 'hot' or 'cold' is about being passionate or indifferent about faith, with 'hot' being good and 'cold' being bad. But would Jesus really prefer us to be 'cold' rather than 'lukewarm' (v. 16)? Does that make any sense? Is open antagonism to faith better than half-hearted acceptance—especially considering how many of us hover around the fringes before making a clear step of commitment?

To hear this the way John's original audience would have heard it, we need to listen with some understanding of life in first-century Laodicea. Founded in the third century BC, it was (like Thyatira) a commercial rather than military city. Cicero (in the first century BC) knew it as a centre of banking, but it was also famous for its textile industry and a cloth made from glossy, black wool. And the physician Galen (from the second century AD) mentions its medical school which produced ear ointment and eye salve. The city was so proud of its financial independence that it refused imperial help for rebuilding after an earthquake in AD60. No wonder they thought they were rich and well clothed, with good eyesight (v. 17)!

The one thing they did not have was a good water supply. Colossae, further up the Lycus Valley, was known for its cold springs. Hierapolis, across the valley, had hot springs and was a prosperous centre for healing and religion. But Laodicea had to bring its water from hot springs further up the mountain, and by the time it reached the city it was lukewarm and full of calcium deposits—enough to make you throw up if you drank it! Cold water is good for refreshment; hot water is good for healing; but lukewarm water is good for nothing—just like the Laodiceans. Jesus' critique was not of their faith but of their lives ('I know your *deeds*': v. 15, my emphasis). Their complacency meant the grace they had received was not being translated into action to transform the world around them.

Yet Jesus still loves them; his offer is still to come and sit with them and put things right—if invited. The path to real victory is through admitting weakness; letting go of pride and inviting Jesus to put things right will lead to sharing his kingdom and throne.

Guidelines

In many ways, the messages to the seven *ekklesiae* are thought to be the most accessible part of the book of Revelation. They are addressed to followers of Jesus like us; though in a different context, we can see they have strengths and weaknesses, as we do. They paint a portrait of who Jesus is, suggest practical action, and remind us of both the responsibilities and the privileges of discipleship. But they also need to be read with understanding. We need to recognise that, even if they are written for us, they are not written to us.

There are plenty of things to think about from each of the messages. Have I lost my first love (Ephesus)? Do I find my wealth and security in God (Smyrna)? Have I stood firm in the face of opposition (Pergamum)? Have I allowed compromise to lure me away from faith (Thyatira)? Am I resting on my laurels (Sardis)? Have I allowed God to remove my fear (Philadelphia)? Am I ready to open the door of my life to Jesus (Laodicea)?

But the messages as a whole, not least the pattern they follow, also offer insight. The vision of Jesus is multifaceted, and different aspects of the truth about him will be relevant in different times and places. What am I learning about Jesus in the stage of life I am now in? Jesus knows all about us—not just our inner thoughts, but how we are living, and the impact we are having on the world around us. While we often focus on our thoughts and intentions, these messages show an interest in action and integrity of life, which is typical of the New Testament as a whole. It is not the person who trots out the right words who will be saved, but 'the one who does the will of my Father who is in heaven' (Matthew 7:21).

These messages are also very realistic about the pressures of discipleship, the challenges from within and without for all Christian communities, and they encourage us to be vigilant. But we are not alone; the one who walks among the lampstands promises his presence and his power, and holds out the prospect of the ultimate reward when we see him face to face.

As we pray for those facing persecution around the world, perhaps we need also to pray for those of us whose chief danger is not persecution but compromise.

FURTHER READING

Ian Paul, *How to Read the Book of Revelation* (Grove Books, 2003).

Craig Koester, *Revelation and the End of All Things* (Eerdmans, 2001).

Michael Gorman, *Reading Revelation Responsibly* (Cascade, 2011).

Ben Witherington III, *Revelation* (New Cambridge Bible Commentary) (Cambridge University Press, 2003).

Supporting BRF
with a gift in your will

Throughout its history, BRF's ministry has been enabled thanks to the generosity of those who have shared its vision and supported its work both by giving during their lifetime and also through legacy gifts.

BRF is a charity that is passionate about making a difference through the Christian faith. We want to see lives and communities transformed through our creative programmes and resources for individuals, churches and schools. We are doing this by resourcing:

- Christian growth and understanding of the Bible by people of all ages through our Bible reading notes, other published resources and events.
- Churches for outreach in the local community through Messy Church, Who Let The Dads Out? and The Gift of Years.
- The teaching of Christianity within primary schools through our Barnabas in Schools programme.
- Children's and family ministry in churches through our websites and published resources.

Legacies make a significant difference to our ability to achieve our purpose. A legacy gift would help fund the development and sustainability of BRF's work into the future. We hope you may consider a gift to help us continue to take this work forward in the decades to come.

For further information about making a gift to BRF in your will or to discuss how a specific bequest could be used to develop our ministry, please contact Sophie Aldred (Head of Fundraising) or Richard Fisher (Chief Executive) by email at fundraising@brf.org.uk or by phone on 01865 319700.

The BRF

Magazine

Journey through Lent   140
Kristina Petersen

Encountering the Risen Christ   142
Mark Bradford

An extract from *Dust and Glory*   144
Mark Bradford

Recommended reading   147
Kevin Ball

Order Forms

Supporting BRF's Ministry   150
BRF Ministry Appeal Response Form   153
BRF Publications   155
Subscriptions   156

Journey through Lent

Kristina Petersen

'I hope you like shortbread,' said my friend. 'I do, but I've given it up for Lent,' was my reply. 'Oh no! I thought you'd only given up chocolate. I bought the shortbread especially for you!' With this, I discovered one of the pitfalls of giving up sweet treats for Lent.

What is the point of Lent? Surely there is more to it than giving up sweets, chocolate, alcohol or Facebook, or even taking up some kind of good habit or reading a Lent book? According to the Oxford English Dictionary, Lent is 'the period preceding Easter, which is devoted to fasting, abstinence, and penitence in commemoration of Christ's fasting in the wilderness. In the Western Church it runs from Ash Wednesday to Holy Saturday, and so includes 40 weekdays.'

What would be true fasting for us—fasting that strips us of the external methods that we use to distract ourselves, which ultimately keep us away from God? Jesus was full of the Holy Spirit and was led by that very same Spirit into the desert, where he was tempted (Luke 4:1–2; see verses 1–13 for the full story). After being affirmed by God and before starting his ministry, he needed to experience a desert time, a time to think about his ministry and his priorities. Stripped of all support systems, hungry and possibly lonely, he was tempted to use some short cuts to reach his aims: after all, what would be wrong with using authority and splendour to reach the world? Surely, throwing himself from the highest point of the temple and allowing angels to rescue him would demonstrate the power of God to those visiting the temple? Jesus, however, not only knew the scriptures but was also listening to his Father and knew his Father's will for him, which did not include doing miracles for their own sake.

What are our temptations when all our support systems are stripped from us? What do we do when things go wrong? Do you reach for the chocolate, a glass of wine, your mobile phone, the computer keyboard or the remote control when you need comfort after a bad day? We all have ways of distracting ourselves and of numbing pain after a difficult experience. This is not wrong in itself but it can prevent us from facing issues and dealing with the source of pain, and it can stop us from turning to God. Why is he not our first port of call when things go wrong?

Jesus is led into the desert because he needs this time before starting his public ministry, before he teaches and heals, before he faces rejection and ridicule. It is a training ground, a necessary preparation for his ministry. What do we need in order to be able to give out and minister to others? Sometimes we need to be forced to come face to face with ourselves and with God. Going on a retreat (without our mobile phones) can do that, but so can going to live as part of a community, working with others for a common goal, or spending time immersed in a different culture. Alternatively, we can simply remove some of our external securities—whatever it is that we use to distract ourselves (TV, books, food, the internet). Who are you when all these things are stripped away? What do you need to give up to become more truly yourself, and to come closer to God?

In fact, what image of God do we have? This may also be something to give up. 'If we're to draw closer to God, we need to be willing to give up some of our entrenched ideas about God in order to see him more clearly… We need to allow the light to be shed on those places where our idea of God is too harsh, too weak, too small, too fragile, too stern (Maggi Dawn, *Giving It Up*, BRF, 2009). Being removed from external distractions can bring us face to face not only with ourselves but also with our image of God. It can enable us to hear more clearly from him, and, when he speaks to us, we may be in for a surprise!

Once we have journeyed through the desert, we are better equipped to reach out to others. 'Is not this the kind of fasting I have chosen: to loose the chains of injustice and untie the cords of the yoke, to set the oppressed free and break every yoke?' (Isaiah 58:6, NIV). If Lent is a time when we focus only on ourselves, it could be quite self-indulgent. Jesus went to Nazareth straight after his time in the desert. There, people rejected him and tried to stone him. Not an easy start to his public ministry! Yet he had been affirmed by his Father and had dealt with some temptations, and he was now ready to speak the truth, regardless of the reaction it would provoke.

What kind of fast does God require of us? What do you need to give up in order to hear him speak to you? What do you then need to take up in order to serve him? Lent can be a time of drawing closer to God, to our true selves and to other people. It can be a journey from the death of old habits to a new way of looking at life.

Oh, and I'll have a piece of that shortbread now, please.

Kristina Petersen is BRF's Editorial Coordinator. She lives in Oxford and is an accomplished linguist, fluent in German, English and Dutch.

Encountering the Risen Christ

Mark Bradford

For a while now, it has struck me as unusual how the church frequently misses the vital importance of Easter. Having been part of a church community all of my life, I remember the 'light-bulb' moment in my late teens when I came to realise that Christmas was not the main event in the church's calendar. I could never have guessed it from mere observation!

As Tom Wright has remarked, 'Take Christmas away, and in biblical terms you lose two chapters at the front of Matthew and Luke, nothing else. Take Easter away, and you don't have a New Testament; you don't have a Christianity' (*Surprised by Hope*, SPCK, 2007, pp. 256–57). So, no resurrection, no Christianity. If nothing really did happen that first Easter, then we pack up and go home. But if something did happen at Easter, then it changes everything.

Of course, this is what the church has always believed. The first apostles saw themselves as witnesses to the resurrection of Jesus. The heart of their message was to teach and proclaim that in Jesus there is resurrection from the dead (Romans 1:4). Sunday, being the day of resurrection, quickly became the day on which Christians gathered to worship the risen Christ together, and, from as early as the second century, the celebration of Easter took place as a season rather than merely a day. This season 'was regarded as a time of rejoicing, and every day was treated in the same way as Sunday—that is, with no kneeling for prayer or fasting' (Paul Bradshaw, *Early Christian Worship*, SPCK, 2010, p. 93).

Yet, in my experience, the contemporary church has lost a vital sense of the importance of Easter. Lent is often kept, with plenty of resources available for this 40-day period that prepares us for Easter, but, inexplicably, we celebrate Easter for only a single day. In the church calendar, Easter is not just a single day; it is a whole season. While Lent is 40 days long, the Easter season is 50. The energy put into our self-denial during Lent should be far outstripped, both in intensity and longevity, by the energy put into feasting and celebration during Easter.

My book, *Encountering the Risen Christ*, emerged out of a course I ran in my own church as a way of encouraging people to mark the Easter season far more intentionally. Over the seven-week period leading to Pentecost, we looked at the encounters that Mary, Thomas, Peter, Cleopas and his companion, and the disciples as a group had with the risen Christ. These encounters are some of the most intimate, striking and transformative stories to be found in the whole of the Bible.

There is a profound difference between a meeting and an encounter.

- Meetings are usually planned and predictable events. Encounters are often unplanned and can have consequences far beyond anything that we can imagine.
- Meetings tend to be fairly superficial affairs in which the 'usual business' is discussed. Encounters are deep affairs in which the agenda is not set by us.
- We can often walk out of meetings largely unaffected by what has happened. We will never leave an encounter unchanged. In fact, we may never to be the same again.

This was certainly the case for Mary, for the disciples, for Thomas, for Cleopas and his companion, and for Peter—as I explore in the book. In each of these stories, we find that the risen Christ shows up in the most ordinary of places and encounters the most ordinary of people, in order to lead them out of dead-end situations of brokenness and into new possibilities for life and healing and hope. And all because of what happened that first Easter Sunday.

Mary would journey with the risen Christ from sadness to hope; the disciples, from fear to confidence; Thomas, from doubt to confirmation; Cleopas and his companion, from shattered dreams to new beginnings; and Peter, from failure to restoration.

In the forthcoming season of Easter—between Easter Day and Pentecost—we are invited not only to listen in to these encounters but also to participate in them ourselves. We, too, have sadness, fear, doubts, shattered dreams and a sense of failure. The risen Christ invites us to journey with him toward fresh possibilities of hope, confidence, confirmation, new beginnings and restoration, because, if something did happen that first Easter, it offers the potential to change everything.

Mark Bradford is the author of Encountering the Risen Christ, *a book for the Easter season. It focuses on the main characters in the post-resurrection accounts, exploring how meeting the risen Christ transforms their lives. To order a copy, please turn to page 155.*

An extract from
Dust and Glory

Dust and Glory, BRF's Lent book for 2016, has been written to accompany you through this special period of prayer and self-examination, a time of turning from winter to spring, from death to life. In this book, the questions are as important as the answers, and may call us to deep heart-searching. Author David Runcorn's goal is to draw us to authentic faith that acknowledges both the dust of our mortality and the glory that keeps breaking in with unexpected life, hope and new beginnings. The following extract, 'Holy laughter', is for the Fourth Sunday of Lent.

> *As the first day of the week was dawning, Mary Magdalene and the other Mary went to see the tomb. And suddenly there was a great earthquake; for an angel of the Lord, descending from heaven, came and rolled back the stone and sat on it... The angel said to the women, 'Do not be afraid; I know that you are looking for Jesus who was crucified. He is not here; for he has been raised, as he said. Come, see the place where he lay. Then go quickly and tell his disciples, "He has been raised from the dead."... So they left the tomb quickly with fear and great joy, and ran to tell his disciples.*
>
> MATTHEW 28:1–2, 5–8 (NRSV)

Stories told too often can easily lose their capacity to surprise. We know them too well. So, when approaching the major seasons of the Christian faith, I pray for one insight or thought to come fresh to me. Last Easter it came in this story, with the angel who 'rolled back the stone and sat on it'—that detail. I can imagine that rolling a heavy stone away on your own would leave you out of breath but I never considered it might be a problem for angels.

Sitting down has a 'job done' feel to it. It is the way we picture Jesus at the right hand of God. Certainly, while the angel is sitting on it, there is no chance that anyone could roll the stone back again. The mood feels teasingly casual, somehow. Something solid enough to seal in death itself is reduced to a handy spot to sit for a moment.

We surely do not suppose that the stone was rolled away to let Jesus out. If death could not hold him, a stone would be no obstacle. Rather, it was rolled away to let us in. There is a discovery for us to make. I fancy the angel fixing me with a mischievous 'You won't believe what I've just seen!' smile. Actually, this morning I think he winked at me! I am trying to pray but I keep giggling.

There is a literary theory that all storytelling revolves around four types of plot, which correspond to the seasons of creation: autumn is tragedy, winter is satire, summer is romance and spring is comedy. Resurrection is a sign of spring-time. New life is emerging after the long death of winter, and this is the season of comedy.

It may be that our most trusting response to the resurrection story is laughter. Let the lawyers and theologians do the serious analysis, but do not miss the angel sitting on that stone watching us all, grinning. How did the angels in the tomb contain themselves, waiting for the first bewildered witnesses. 'Shh, they're coming!' Well, wouldn't you, on a day like that?

The poet Anne Sexton was often left bruised in her pilgrimage through faith and life, but in one of her most moving poems she imagines meeting up with God, who surprises her by producing a pack of cards and playing poker with

> *It may be that our most trusting response to the resurrection story is laughter*

her. She is dealt a hand, as, in a sense, we all are in this life. We make what we can of what we find in our grasp. To her surprise, it is a very strong hand. She thinks she has won. Then God trumps her with a fifth ace! He cheats—he breaks the rules—but her response is not outrage. She loves it! The poem ends with the poet and God doubled over each other in helpless laughter at their 'double triumphs' ('The rowing endeth' in *The Complete Poems*, Houghton Mifflin, 1982, pp. 473–74).

I once invited a prayer group to silently imagine they were entering the court of God the king. They were to draw near with whatever expressions of reverence they felt appropriate. The mood was serious until someone suddenly laughed out loud. I asked afterwards what had happened. 'Well, you know when you are in the presence of someone really important, you feel awkward and tongue-tied and they say something to relax you?'

'Yes,' I said.'

'Well, God told me a joke.'

There is an important tradition, in many older societies, of the clown or jester. In royal courts, among religious dignitaries and in the marketplaces, they have permission to mock the pomposity of the powerful and dethrone the self-important. They laugh at the po-faced solemnity that we confuse with reverence. They simply refuse to take us seriously—and that is their gift. Their laughter relativises the powers. They roll large and important stones away and just sit on them.

This is the season of comedy. Resurrection is God's fifth ace. He has broken the rules. You just have to laugh, don't you?

Prayer: Lord, teach me to trust enough to laugh.

David Runcorn is a popular writer, speaker, teacher, retreat leader and spiritual guide. His books include The Spirituality Workbook: a guide for pilgrims, explorers and seekers *and* Fear and Trust: God-centred leadership. *He lives in Gloucester, where he is involved with the selection, training and support of people called to Christian ministry of all kinds.*

To order a copy of this book, please turn to page 155. Alternatively, it is available at Christian bookshops.

Recommended reading

Kevin Ball

Encouragement and hope—two words that can brighten even the darkest of days. It is said that, to feel positive, creative and motivated about ourselves, we need to hear five encouraging comments to every one critical comment. If that is what we need in the ordinary, more stable days of life, then our needs during the darker seasons of life multiply the importance of these special words many times over.

The best way to encourage someone, of course, is to be right there alongside them in person, but the busy, demanding aspects of life often make this impossible. It's in these cases that an encouraging gift may be just what is needed. January 2016 sees the publication of two new gift books of encouragement and hope.

The Recovery of Hope
Bible reflections for sensing God's presence and hearing God's call
Naomi Starkey

pb, 978 0 85746 417 0, 144 pages, £8.99

Naomi Starkey, editor of *New Daylight* for the last 15 years, has brought together, in her new book *The Recovery of Hope*, a selection of her own *New Daylight* readings covering these themes, along with some newly written poems of reflection.

Naomi writes, 'As I reviewed my contributions to *New Daylight*, I found that I have been drawn to a recognisable pattern of themes that related to my pilgrimage of faith: the hunger for God's consoling presence especially during hard times, the challenge to respond to his call on my life, and the discovery—and rediscovery, again and again—of the deep reassurance that I am not only known but loved beyond understanding.

'So I have woven these Bible readings into a kind of journey towards the recovery of hope, the hope of experiencing first-hand the utter sufficiency of God's grace, love and forgiveness, a hope that we may know with our heads for a while—perhaps even a long while—before we truly feel it in our hearts. It is the hope of knowing God not only as consoling presence in the darkness but in the challenge of responding to his call and in the transformative experience of knowing how much we are his beloved children.'

Postcards from Heaven
Words and pictures to help you hear from God
Ellie Hart
pb, 978 0 85746 427 9, 160 pages, £7.99

Postcards from Heaven, by a new author to BRF, Ellie Hart, combines beautiful pastel artwork with brief but deeply touching reflections of encouragement and hope on the seasons of life.

Ellie writes, 'We all live in a season of one kind or another, a season of work, a season of ministry, a season of looking after children, a season of joy, a season of grieving, seasons of friendship and relationships. The main feature of seasons is that they don't last forever: the place we move into next will be different in many ways.

'Last summer, a friend of mine who hears God more clearly, perhaps, than anyone else I know came and told me that the Father wanted me to write a book about the seasons that we go through in life, especially about how to get through the tougher seasons and how to navigate those curious empty spaces that come in between seasons of activity.

'So I've done my best, and my heart's desire is that this book could become a place where you encounter our wonderful, beautiful, untameable, passionate, loving God and hear him speak directly to you in whatever circumstance you find yourself in.'

Immeasurably more...

Every time I stand on the beach I scoop up as much water as I can hold in my hands and I think, 'This is how much of God's presence, power and peace I have experienced so far.' Then I look out at the sea. The difference between the water I can hold in my hands and the contents of the Mediterranean Sea (and then the Atlantic Ocean) is beyond my ability to comprehend. That's how much more there is to explore of God; that's how much more he has for you. You just need to ask (page 69).

A Christian Guide to Environmental Issues
Martin J. Hodson and Margot R. Hodson

pb, 978 0 85746 383 8, 224 pages £9.99

Encouragement and hope are two qualities that husband and wife authors Margot and Martin Hodson are anxious to find in the deeply concerning issues relating to planet earth's environment and its ongoing ability to support life.

A Christian Guide to Environmental Issues explains the issues, not focusing just on global warming but also examining:

- biodiversity and the loss of many animal species because of the activities of humans—a process now being termed the sixth great extinction event.
- the pressure on clean water supplies. This is best illustrated by the fact that the amount of fresh water available today is pretty much as it was 2000 years ago, but today the world's population is 7 billion and still growing—not the 250 million of the time of Jesus.
- the provision of energy to supply businesses and homes, the impact of fossil fuels on the environment and the slow development of and opposition to alternative energy systems.
- the continued focus by governments on economic growth driven by increased consumption, seeming to ignore the fact that the world's natural resources are limited. If the world's precious natural resources were shared sustainably and equally among its population today, we would all need to adopt the lifestyle of a country such as the Sudan.

What can we actually do? Environmental experts Margot and Martin not only lead you through the facts and figures but help you to explore the issues from a biblical point of view, showing the importance of the creation in God's redemptive plan and our responsibility in its management.

This book is ideal for church groups or individuals wanting to explore the issues intelligently and get involved. Communities will need to come together, understand the realities, accept the lifestyle changes required and then effectively lobby to encourage political leaders to prioritise the issues, so that a much-needed hope can be realised.

To find out more, to read sample chapters and to order online, visit www. brfonline.org.uk. Alternatively you can order using the form on page 155.

As a Christian charity, BRF is involved in eight complementary areas.

- **BRF** (www.brf.org.uk) resources adults for their spiritual journey through Bible reading notes, books and Quiet Days. BRF also provides the infrastructure that supports our other specialist ministries.
- **Foundations21** (www.foundations21.net) provides flexible and innovative ways for individuals and groups to explore their Christian faith and discipleship through a multimedia internet-based resource.
- **Messy Church** (www.messychurch.org.uk), led by Lucy Moore, enables churches all over the UK (and increasingly abroad) to reach children and adults beyond the fringes of the church.
- **Barnabas in Churches** (www.barnabasinchurches.org.uk) helps churches to support, resource and develop their children's ministry with the under-11s more effectively .
- **Barnabas in Schools** (www.barnabasinschools.org.uk) enables primary school children and teachers to explore Christianity creatively and bring the Bible alive within RE and Collective Worship.
- **Faith in Homes** (www.faithinhomes.org.uk) supports families to explore and live out the Christian faith at home.
- **Who Let The Dads Out** (www.wholetthedadsout.org) inspires churches to engage with dads and their pre-school children.
- **The Gift of Years** (www.brf.org.uk/thegiftofyears) celebrates the blessings of long life and seeks to meet the spiritual needs of older people.

At the heart of BRF's ministry is a desire to equip adults and children for Christian living—helping them to read and understand the Bible, explore prayer and grow as disciples of Jesus. We need your help to make an impact on the local church, local schools and the wider community.

- You could support BRF's ministry with a one-off gift or regular donation (using the response form on page 153).
- You could consider making a bequest to BRF in your will.
- You could encourage your church to support BRF as part of your church's giving to home mission—perhaps focusing on a specific area of our ministry, or a particular member of our Barnabas team.
- Most important of all, you could support BRF with your prayers.

If you would like to discuss how a specific gift or bequest could be used in the development of our ministry, please phone 01865 319700 or email enquiries@brf.org.uk.

Whatever you can do or give, we thank you for your support.

HOW TO ENCOURAGE BIBLE READING IN YOUR CHURCH

BRF has been helping individuals connect with the Bible for over 90 years. We want to support churches as they seek to encourage church members into regular Bible reading.

Order a Bible reading resources pack

This pack is designed to give your church the tools to publicise our Bible reading notes. It includes:

- Sample Bible reading notes for your congregation to try.
- Publicity resources, including a poster.
- A church magazine feature about Bible reading notes.

The pack is free, but we welcome a £5 donation to cover the cost of postage. If you require a pack to be sent outside the UK or require a specific number of sample Bible reading notes, please contact us for postage costs. More information about what the current pack contains is available on our website.

How to order and find out more

- Visit **www.biblereadingnotes.org.uk/for-churches/**
- Telephone BRF on 01865 319700 between 9.15 am and 5.30 pm.
- Write to us at BRF, 15 The Chambers, Vineyard, Abingdon, OX14 3FE

Keep informed about our latest initiatives

We are continuing to develop resources to help churches encourage people into regular Bible reading, wherever they are on their journey. Join our email list at **www.biblereadingnotes.org.uk/helpingchurches/** to stay informed about the latest initiatives that your church could benefit from.

Introduce a friend to our notes

We can send information about our notes and current prices for you to pass on. Please contact us.

GUIDELINES SUBSCRIPTIONS

Please note our subscription rates 2016–2017. From the May 2016 issue, the new subscription rates will be:

Individual subscriptions covering 3 issues for under 5 copies, payable in advance (including postage and packing):

	UK	Eur/Economy	Airmail
GUIDELINES each set of 3 p.a.	£16.35	£24.90	£28.20
GUIDELINES 3-year sub (i.e. 9 issues)	£43.20	N/A	N/A

Group subscriptions covering 3 issues for 5 copies or more, sent to ONE UK address (post free).

GUIDELINES   £13.05   each set of 3 p.a.

Overseas group subscription rates available on request.
Contact enquiries@brf.org.uk.

Please note that the annual billing period for Group Subscriptions runs from 1 May to 30 April.

Copies of the notes may also be obtained from Christian bookshops:

GUIDELINES   £4.35 each copy

Visit www.biblereadingnotes.org.uk for information about our other Bible reading notes and Apple apps for iPhone and iPod touch.

GL0116

BRF MINISTRY APPEAL RESPONSE FORM

I would like to help BRF. Please use my gift for:
❑ Where most needed   ❑ Barnabas Children's Ministry   ❑ Messy Church
❑ Who Let The Dads Out?   ❑ The Gift of Years
Please complete all relevant sections of this form and print clearly.

Title ____ First name/initials _____ Surname _____
Address _____
_____ Postcode _____
Telephone _____ Email _____

Regular giving

If you would like to give by direct debit, please tick the box below and fill in details:

❑ I would like to make a regular gift of £ _____ per month / quarter / year
(delete as appropriate) by Direct Debit. (Please complete the form on page 159.)

If you would like to give by standing order, please contact Priscilla Kew (tel: 01235 462305; email priscilla.kew@brf.org.uk; write to BRF address below).

One-off donation

Please accept my special gift of
❑ £10 ❑ £50 ❑ £100 (other) £ _____ by

❑ Cheque / Charity Voucher payable to 'BRF'
❑ Visa / Mastercard / Charity Card
(delete as appropriate)

Name on card _____

Card no. ❑❑❑❑ ❑❑❑❑ ❑❑❑❑ ❑❑❑❑

Start date ❑❑❑❑   **Expiry date** ❑❑❑❑

Security code ❑❑❑

Signature _____ Date _____

❑ I would like to give a legacy to BRF. Please send me further information.

❑ I want BRF to claim back tax on this gift.
(If you tick this box, please fill in gift aid declaration overleaf.)

Please detach and send this completed form to: BRF, 15 The Chambers, Vineyard, Abingdon OX14 3FE.   BRF is a Registered Charity (No.233280)

Bible Reading Fellowship

Please treat as Gift Aid donations all qualifying gifts of money made:

today ☐   in the past 4 years ☐   in the future ☐

I confirm I have paid or will pay an amount of Income Tax and/or Capital Gains Tax for each tax year (6 April to 5 April) that is at least equal to the amount of tax that all the charities that I donate to will reclaim on my gifts for that tax year. I understand that other taxes such as VAT or Council Tax do not qualify. I understand that BRF will reclaim 25p of tax on every £1 that I give.

☐   My donation does not qualify for Gift Aid.

Signature _____

Date _____

Notes:

1. Please notify BRF if you want to cancel this declaration, change your name or home address, or no longer pay sufficient tax on your income and/or capital gains.

2. If you pay Income Tax at the higher/additional rate and want to receive the additional tax relief due to you, you must include all your Gift Aid donations on your Self-Assessment tax return or ask HM Revenue and Customs to adjust your tax code.

BRF PUBLICATIONS ORDER FORM

Please send me the following book(s):	Quantity	Price	Total
428 6 Encountering the Risen Christ (M. Bradford)	_____	£7.99	_____
357 9 Dust and Glory (D. Runcorn)	_____	£7.99	_____
417 0 The Recovery of Hope (N. Starkey)	_____	£7.99	_____
427 9 Postcards from Heaven (E. Hart)	_____	£7.99	_____
383 8 Christian Guide Environmental (M.&M. Hodson)	_____	£9.99	_____
680 1 Giving It Up (M. Dawn)	_____	£7.99	_____
Quiet Spaces sample copy	_____	FREE	_____

Total cost of books £ _____
Donation £ _____
Postage and packing £ _____
TOTAL £ _____

POSTAGE AND PACKING CHARGES				
Order value	UK	Europe	Economy (Surface)	Standard (Air)
Under £7.00	£1.25	£3.00	£3.50	£5.50
£7.00–£29.99	£2.25	£5.50	£6.50	£10.00
£30.00 and over	free	prices on request		

Please complete the payment details below and send with payment to: **BRF, 15 The Chambers, Vineyard, Abingdon OX14 3FE**

Name _____

Address _____

_____ Postcode _____

Tel _____ Email _____

Total enclosed £ _____ (cheques should be made payable to 'BRF')

Please charge my Visa ☐ Mastercard ☐ Switch card ☐ with £ _____

Card no: ☐☐☐☐☐☐☐☐☐☐☐☐☐☐☐☐☐☐

Expires ☐☐☐☐ Security code ☐☐☐

Issue no (Switch only) ☐☐☐☐

Signature (essential if paying by credit/Switch) _____

GUIDELINES INDIVIDUAL SUBSCRIPTIONS

❏ I would like to take out a subscription myself:

Your name _____

Your address _____

_____ Postcode _____

Tel _____ Email _____

Please send *Guidelines* beginning with the May 2016 / September 2016 /
January 2017 issue: (delete as applicable)

(please tick box)	UK	Europe/Economy	Airmail
GUIDELINES	❏ £16.35	❏ £24.90	❏ £28.20
GUIDELINES 3-year sub	❏ £43.20		
GUIDELINES PDF download	❏ £13.05 (UK and overseas)		

Please complete the payment details below and send with appropriate
payment to: **BRF, 15 The Chambers, Vineyard, Abingdon OX14 3FE**

Total enclosed £ _____ (cheques should be made payable to 'BRF')

Please charge my Visa ❏ Mastercard ❏ Switch card ❏ with £ _____

Card no: ☐☐☐☐☐☐☐☐☐☐☐☐☐☐☐☐☐☐

Expires ☐☐☐☐ Security code ☐☐☐

Issue no (Switch only) ☐☐☐☐

Signature (essential if paying by card) _____

To set up a direct debit, please also complete the form on page 159 and send
it to BRF with this form.

BRF is a Registered Charity

GUIDELINES GIFT SUBSCRIPTIONS

❏ I would like to give a gift subscription (please provide both names and addresses:

Your name _____

Your address _____

_____ Postcode _____

Tel _____ Email _____

Gift subscription name _____

Gift subscription address _____

_____ Postcode _____

Gift message (20 words max. or include your own gift card for the recipient)

_____

_____

Please send *Guidelines* beginning with the May 2016 / September 2016 / January 2017 issue: (delete as applicable)

(please tick box)	UK	Europe/Economy	Airmail
GUIDELINES	❏ £16.35	❏ £24.90	❏ £28.20
GUIDELINES 3-year sub	❏ £43.20		
GUIDELINES PDF download	❏ £13.05 (UK and overseas)		

Please complete the payment details below and send with appropriate payment to: **BRF, 15 The Chambers, Vineyard, Abingdon OX14 3FE**

Total enclosed £ _____ (cheques should be made payable to 'BRF')

Please charge my Visa ❏ Mastercard ❏ Switch card ❏ with £ _____

Card no: ⬚⬚⬚⬚ ⬚⬚⬚⬚ ⬚⬚⬚⬚ ⬚⬚⬚⬚ ⬚⬚⬚⬚

Expires ⬚⬚⬚⬚ Security code ⬚⬚⬚

Issue no (Switch only) ⬚⬚⬚⬚

Signature (essential if paying by card) _____

To set up a direct debit, please also complete the form on page 159 and send it to BRF with this form.

DIRECT DEBIT PAYMENTS

Now you can pay for your annual subscription to BRF notes using Direct Debit. You need only give your bank details once, and the payment is made automatically every year until you cancel it. If you would like to pay by Direct Debit, please use the form opposite, entering your BRF account number under 'Reference'.

You are fully covered by the Direct Debit Guarantee:

The Direct Debit Guarantee

- This Guarantee is offered by all banks and building societies that accept instructions to pay Direct Debits.
- If there are any changes to the amount, date or frequency of your Direct Debit, The Bible Reading Fellowship will notify you 10 working days in advance of your account being debited or as otherwise agreed. If you request The Bible Reading Fellowship to collect a payment, confirmation of the amount and date will be given to you at the time of the request.
- If an error is made in the payment of your Direct Debit, by The Bible Reading Fellowship or your bank or building society, you are entitled to a full and immediate refund of the amount paid from your bank or building society.
  - – If you receive a refund you are not entitled to, you must pay it back when The Bible Reading Fellowship asks you to.
- You can cancel a Direct Debit at any time by simply contacting your bank or building society. Written confirmation may be required. Please also notify us.

The Bible Reading Fellowship

Instruction to your bank or building society to pay by Direct Debit

Please fill in the whole form using a ballpoint pen and send to The Bible Reading Fellowship, 15 The Chambers, Vineyard, Abingdon OX14 3FE.

Service User Number: | 5 | 5 | 8 | 2 | 2 | 9 |

Name and full postal address of your bank or building society

To: The Manager	Bank/Building Society
Address	
	Postcode

Name(s) of account holder(s)

| |

Branch sort code

| | | | | | |

Bank/Building Society account number

| | | | | | | | | |

Reference

| | | | | | | | |

Instruction to your Bank/Building Society

Please pay The Bible Reading Fellowship Direct Debits from the account detailed in this instruction, subject to the safeguards assured by the Direct Debit Guarantee.
I understand that this instruction may remain with The Bible Reading Fellowship and, if so, details will be passed electronically to my bank/building society.

Signature(s)	
Date	

Banks and Building Societies may not accept Direct Debit instructions for some types of account.

This page is intentionally left blank.